T0131582

THE BOOK
OF LIFE

AN OWNER'S MANUAL

Copyright © 2021 Larry Heisler, M.A., LMT.

All rights reserved. No part of this book may be used or reproduced by any means, graphic, electronic, or mechanical, including photocopying, recording, taping or by any information storage retrieval system without the written permission of the author except in the case of brief quotations embodied in critical articles and reviews.

Balboa Press books may be ordered through booksellers or by contacting:

Balboa Press
A Division of Hay House
1663 Liberty Drive
Bloomington, IN 47403
www.balboapress.com
844-682-1282

Because of the dynamic nature of the Internet, any web addresses or links contained in this book may have changed since publication and may no longer be valid. The views expressed in this work are solely those of the author and do not necessarily reflect the views of the publisher, and the publisher hereby disclaims any responsibility for them.

The author of this book does not dispense medical advice or prescribe the use of any technique as a form of treatment for physical, emotional, or medical problems without the advice of a physician, either directly or indirectly. The intent of the author is only to offer information of a general nature to help you in your quest for emotional and spiritual well-being. In the event you use any of the information in this book for yourself, which is your constitutional right, the author and the publisher assume no responsibility for your actions.

Artistic Director: David Derr

Print information available on the last page.

Scripture quotations are taken from the Holy Bible, King James Version (Public Domain)

ISBN: 978-1-9822-7757-4 (sc)
ISBN: 978-1-9822-7759-8 (hc)
ISBN: 978-1-9822-7758-1 (e)

Library of Congress Control Number: 2021923753

Balboa Press rev. date: 02/26/2022

THE BOOK
OF LIFE

AN OWNER'S MANUAL

LARRY HEISLER, M.A., LMT

BALBOA.PRESS
A DIVISION OF HAY HOUSE

MY STORY

I was born in the year of the Water Dragon. My birth-date numerology is a twenty-two. I have two *"fingers of fate"* in my astrological chart. If you know what I just said, you also know why this book exists.

I venture to see the anatomized spirit in all creation. According to the Gospel of Thomas (77b), Jesus said, *"Split wood, I am there. Lift up a rock, you will find me there."*

I feel supported by the quantum physics explanation that all earthly existence is made of light, moving at different frequencies. Nikola Tesla said, *"Everything is light."* Physicists might call it electromagnetic force. Pig Pen of the Grateful Dead sang about it, *"let it shine, let it shine, let it shine!"*

I share Bartholdi's vision of the Goddess of Light. In French she is called "La Deesse` de la Lumiere". It is her we draw our strength from. He created her in his exquisite gift to America, our beloved Statue of Liberty. He saw the goddess in his dreams. I see her in my meditation. I keep a throne for her in my heart.

I believe the adage that a pig uses 4% of its brain, a human 6%. If being only two percent smarter than a pig is not humbling enough, consider that the Dalai Lama was born in the year of the pig.

I am humbled by the Native American Churches' sacred respect for all of the Mother's Creation, our holy Mother Earth. I honor those that speak on her behalf.

I study the Taoist perspective; "My father is a motion and a rest," and "When you balance your left hand from your right, your right hand from your left, the Kingdom of Heaven shall be open unto thee." I try to live within the Tao Te Ching, but sometimes the biblical mandates of alpha and omega get in the way.

Today, I label myself Interfaith, but as soon as I capitalize its first letter, "I," I have an epiphany of James Joycian magnitude. Joyce called it "quiddities," P.T. Barnum had a different definition.

I just as easily flip for Krishnamurti's perspective that all labels make us definable, tangible, solid, and thereby self-limiting. He advocated "no tribe", Hilda Charlton, meditation master, advocated a tribe of one. As she put it, *"You and God are a majority."*

Chogyam Trungpa Rinpoche sums it up nicely when he says, *"It's easy to be enlightened when there are flush toilets."* That goes double for sushi!

I toy with Carlos Castaneda's Yaqui Indian shaman-sorcerer Don Juan Matus when he exclaims that anonymity in action transforms both the world and us. I revere Castaneda's ability to follow his teacher's directive so beautifully. I also think Francis Bacon's creation of Shakespeare was one of the world's greatest anonymous feats. A brilliant act, a tour de force for all time.

You are about to take a spiritual journey you will not recover from.
And....... you are about to discover your own inner electricity.

A word of Caution: Electricity can be used to feed us and illuminate us, to make toast, or make music.

It can also be used for capital punishment.
Use it with the wisdom of Ben Franklin and you will keep yourself from frying.
Remember, God talks to us through other people.

Oh, one last thing......**If you open the pages herein, you can never go back to feigning ignorance.**

WHAT THIS BOOK IS ABOUT
AND HOW TO USE IT

I have been teaching since 1972.

Everything and anything that was inspirational. It was always a quest, a search for the higher road, the missing chord.

I was blessed to be educated at great NYC schools; my spiritual mentors were some of the most influential teachers of the twentieth century. To this day, I try and leave each person I meet with an inspiration.

After a lifetime of reading voraciously, I'm still looking for that ONE exceptional source that explains things, a cookbook of life. You know when you buy a new car, it comes with an owner's manual.

Need information about the new car?

It's in the book.

Should be the same with humans.

When you are born, you get a book, a BOOK THAT EXPLAINS EVERYTHING!

This would be the one book that I can hand a person and honestly say, "Read this, and you'll get it."

So, this book was created to be an owner's manual for humans. It is a spiritual text that will directly answer why you are here and get this...how to fulfill your life's purpose and destiny. Yeah, big stuff.

YOU WILL STILL HAVE TO WALK THE PATH but at least you will have a roadmap and compass.

The Commandments in the book are supported with lessons accentuated with true life stories.

Like spiritual parables of old, they are teeming with inspiration and drenched in wonder and spirit.

As my spiritual mentor, the meditation master, Hilda Charlton often reminded us, *"Cubby hole your opinions for a time kids, let its energy interact with you and see what comes of it. If it rings true deep down*, then embrace it with an inner eye and an open heart."

She was also fond of saying, *"Eat these words, digest them, and put them directly into action."*

TABLE OF CONTENTS

IN THE BEGINNING

One of Larry's amazing lifelong friends, Aaron, was at a Renaissance gathering in another state. When walking through the festival, there was a place where the psychics, mediums, and gifted intuitive's were performing readings. It was there that Aaron was approached by one of the practitioners.

As he walked by her, she politely asked, *"Do you have a friend named Larry?"*

Aaron responded with a smile, *"Why, yes, and how is it that you know this?"*

The intuitive continued, *"I am getting a powerfully strong message, you are to help him achieve his vision."*

Aaron said, *"Can you tell me more?"*

Her response was simply, *"They have been watching him; he is bringing to Earth a New Energetic."*

PROLOGUE

When my brother Richie came back from India in the early 1970s, he was hip, smart, and filled with inspiration.

With his encouragement and guidance, my spiritual vision blossomed as a teenager. In those early days, my exploration in consciousness was surrounded by what seemed to be fantastic, even miraculous events.

Synchronicity seems to abound when an individual shifts focus from being an observer, routinely playing victim, to a participant in their own growth experience. It's a dramatic realization, with the light bulb turning on in your head, **when you realize that the purpose of life is to GROW and the whole Universe, your whole world is in on it. Growth, that is, your growth.**

As in, an Interactive Universe.

Yes, you heard me correctly.

It's all about you and your personal, spiritual evolution.

The time for Rip Van Winkle is over.

I know you don't remember BUT YOU signed up for this.

Lot of lessons, big school...

When something hits you in the head, like a revelation, in Zen it is referred to as Satori.

Hilda liked to call it, *"An instant shock of God awakening!"* **That's where you are at...**

In 1973, I remember reading a story in a magazine about consciousness. The magazine was called "The New Age Journal". The article had a picture and story of an extraordinary spiritual teacher and healer in lower New York City.

She went by the name Hilda. Nothing more, simply Hilda. I recall saying to myself, *"Now that's refreshing..., in a world inundated with swamis, sensei's, shamans, babas and booboos, There's a Hilda!"*

As I read the article and viewed her picture, I was moved by her deep orbited eyes and her beautiful words of love and spiritual mastery. I made a mental note of her name and quickly moved along with my day.

At least a year went by. I was at home reading a local NYC paper called "The Village Voice", when my angel showed up again. An article about a charismatic woman named Hilda. The article stated, Hilda taught the meditative healing arts in downtown NYC at a church named St. Luke's. Over a hundred people would crowd into a small, almost claustrophobic room, to hear and be in this woman's presence. Some were calling her *"a healing saint,"* others, *"a reservoir of love."*

By this time in my life, I was firmly grounded into meditation and yoga. And once again, I was moved by what this woman had to say in the Voice column. But college, work, a rock band, a girlfriend, left little time in the day. I soon forgot about Hilda and continued my practice and studies. Another year flew by and now I was working as a teacher and in graduate school, both fulltime.

One Thursday, in the Fall of `75, my Brooklyn girlfriend called me excitedly to announce that she was going with friends to a spiritual meditation class in the Village.

To which I replied,
"Don't tell me, you are going to Hilda's class?"
Surprised, she exclaimed,
"How did you know that?"

I simply said,
"I read about her. Call me tomorrow and tell me all about it."

The next day her excitement was all consuming.

So, the following Thursday, I was there, sitting on the cold concrete floor in the center of a room in the church basement. The space was overcrowded, elbow to elbow, and knee to knee. The audience was diverse—suits, hippies, young and old. There was a makeshift band oddly leading both Hindu chants and western gospel songs. Some people were singing, others meditating, and others had their eyes closed, tuning into their breath. A variety of incenses filled the air as in an open Indian bazaar. I was trying to take in the global feel of the place, but this scene had no reference file in my experiences. Suddenly, a serious hush came over the space as an older lady in a sky-blue Indian sari entered the room.

As she made her way up to the front, she casually touched people on their foreheads with an occasional bang on the chest. This was undoubtedly Hilda Charlton.

The seated crowd parted, leaving an aisle for her. She moved with an air of royalty, a dignity with a graceful sweetness about her. She sat in a comfortable chair reading letters and prayer requests from the audience.

Once settled, Hilda stood and raised her hands.

She was graceful, a life-long professional dancer.

Her arms rose expressively, with conviction, as if she were dancing a tango and suddenly the crowd sat upright with a focused attention.

Hilda began,

"Let's make a miracle happen tonight kids!
It's time to use your God given powers.
Close your eyes for a few seconds.
Pull inside....and get quiet......breathe...
now get firm like a master soul."

We sat for just a few minutes, but it seemed to me like an eternity. Hilda then cut the silence,

"Now hold your center, for the rest of the evening kids.
Let's Om, and build up the vibratory rate in here, shall we?"

A chorus of sacred sound rose as Hilda conducted the special invocation of AUM. Raising her arms out-stretched again, she shook her hands intensely, sending her blessing out upon the crowd.

It was a shower of love vibration and the audience lapped it up as if suckling at the feet of the Divine Mother.

From there, the class took off. At least for me.

I cannot exactly tell you what went on, my mind was a rush of thoughts and impulses.

By the break, I had overloaded. This was just so foreign, so different than anything I had ever experienced or expected.

I grabbed my coat and slinked out, fully intending to blow off the rest of the evening.

On my way, I stopped in the lavatory.

I was standing at the vertical commode, reflecting and dazed by what I had just experienced, when a very colorfully dressed individual named Ganesh engaged me in a one-way conversation.

"You can't leave just yet",
Ganesh whispered with an impish smile.
"You've come this far;
Hilda's meditation is extraordinary,
please...do yourself a favor, and stay."

With that intervention, I returned to my floor space.

The lights were dimmed, soft singing began, and Hilda led the group in breathing and visualization.

Her words were soft, inviting,

"From the top of your head to the tip of your toes,
Visualize a golden light.
See it kids, feel it, let it surround you, envelop you...
Now as if there was a nose in the center of your chest,
breathe into your heart center this moment.
On every breath, breathe in this golden healing light.
You are made in the image and likeness of God;
there can be no imperfection in you because
here is no imperfection in God.
I want you to believe in a miracle tonight kids.
Believe in a miracle with all your heart and soul".

Hilda took all of us on an incredible journey. She invoked deities, saints, and angels,
and directed them to bless us;

"In the name of Jesus,
in the name of holy lady Ammal,
in the name of Sai Baba,
touch these spiritual children tonight."

She sweet talked with God, petitioning passionately, lovingly on our behalf.

As I delved deeper and deeper inside, my head swelled with a golden luminosity. I heard Hilda's voice drawing nearer.

The smell of roses washed over me like a wave and suddenly her voice seemed directly in my head.

I felt an astonishing heat emanate up my spine and around my heart and then my forehead exploded, melting into light.

I don't know how long I was stiff in meditation.

When I became conscious, I was the last one in the room.

That is all except for Ganesh, the magical gnome that I met in the lavatory. He was smiling while sweeping around me with a broom. I looked up, astonished. All he said was,

"Hilda's waiting outside for you".

When I got outside, Hilda smiled at me lovingly and said,

"First time kid?" I nodded sheepishly.

She looked me up and down, as if she were reading my insides and then said,

"I only invite a person to my class three times.
You might find it a little strange at first, just give it a couple
of sessions and see if it's something you'll benefit from."

Then she opened her sari-covered arms like a butterfly, hugged me and sent me on my way, numb, blessed and completely dumbfounded.

It was an invitation that took me years to accept, with no hard-sell and no money exchanged.

From that moment on, I was one of "Hilda's kids."

Her generosity of spirit, her generosity with her love and time, were unparalleled. She was an open vessel and we found ourselves in a real spiritual finishing school. Hilda's only request of us was that we give away our love and service as generously and freely as she gave it to us.

Here's what I know from personally making the wrong decisions repeatedly when I was younger. This is a planet of yin and yang. Chinese philosophy says from the one Great Spirit come two opposing forces. Infra-red/ultraviolet, left/right, motion/rest, good and evil, light/dark. It's like there's a vested interest to keep things down here chaotic. Seems to make for good growth. So, whenever you're about to make a real positive change, a step towards the Light, the dark side will put up roadblocks to keep you from coming into your power and fulfilling your destiny. You must dive deep inside yourself to find your spiritually connected inner voice. It takes an awful lot of practice before you will find it.

Once you connect with this inner source of wisdom, it will guide you on your path throughout the rest of your life. You will almost always know what's real and what's phony baloney.

There are things I'm going to share that might make you scratch your head or even press your buttons. Before you say it's B.S., try to discern whether the negative reaction is coming from a lifetime of conditioning and ego or coming from the all-knowing place. Because as soon as the ego hears it cannot be in control, being the lower animal self/dark side, it will protest in your head. It's normal for ego to try and maintain security and control. Letting go of lifelong programming, whatever it might entail, is difficult. Our lower nature wants to believe it has the right to its anger or revenge.

It routinely plays VICTIM. Like a child wanting its way, it will react. This is not in your best interest. The lower ego is a big baby throwing a temper tantrum.

THE PURPOSE OF LIFE
A LIFE CHANGING MESSAGE

Many years ago, **I was privileged** to meet an extraordinary woman. She was only in her twenties with the maturity of a wise, old owl. Hemophilia is a rare **blood disease** that usually occurs in males. Even though it is extremely rare for women to be born with the condition, my friend had it. With the backdrop of a crackling summer evening campfire on Martha's Vineyard, she began to tell me her **amazing story**...

"You know Larry, death does not exist", she quipped as if it were a matter of fact.

She then began to weave a story of how she had witnessed her own near-death experience.

"I am a long-distance runner. It's my therapy, my church. One afternoon, I was running through the park in Queens. I wasn't paying attention and tripped on a rock along the path and slammed my side up against a large boulder. Unbeknownst to me, I had severed my spleen and in short order collapsed, unconscious on the running trail. Other running friends came along. Knowing me and my personal story, I was rushed to the emergency room. Lying on the gurney, unconscious, I slipped out of my physical body.
Standing there, unseen by those around me, in what could best be described as "my light body" or spiritual form, I watched the whole frenzied scene unfold. The emergency room staff was professional and well equipped. The attending physician barked orders to the staff in a mad attempt to save my life. One of workers tried to break the room's tension by mentioning it was a "full moon."

I heard and saw... everything.

After much ado, the doctor whispered, 'she's gone,' except I was not. After some time, I found myself traveling down a bluish gray tunnel. Upon my arrival, to the "other side," deceased members of my family were eagerly awaiting. My grandparents were there! My dog! A favorite uncle, aunts, a dear family friend, my first parakeet and the corner barber who would come out of his shop in the afternoons to give me a lollipop as I walked home from school.

*This was **a reunion filled with incredible happiness and joy, crying and hugging.** I was free, but still felt my humanity connected to the body lying in the hospital bed below. After the reunion period, **I felt drawn, even beckoned to a Light in the distance.** As I moved closer to what can only be described as a tangible force, **my life began to unfold in my mind.** Almost immediately, I began to understand how I became who I was.*

A new awareness came over me and then, a second later, I found myself surrounded and enveloped by that blinding Light. Perhaps more like an incredible loving wholeness, *it was like being embraced in God's arms.*

*Then telepathically, **in my mind's ear,** I heard two questions:*

"What did you learn?" and... "Whom did you help?"

As I wrapped my head around these questions, I inwardly heard,

*`**Your work is yet unfinished, you must return.........***'*

Immediately, I found myself again on the move, traveling, returning, past my loved ones, down the bluish gray tunnel, into the hospital building, into the hospital room, into the hospital bed, and slam back into my body! I was the miracle comeback story of the month. On my way out, I asked to leave via the emergency room, so I would connect with the team that saved my life. I was holding court with the staff members and mentioned to them that they should watch what they say even when the patient is unconscious.

When I repeated the 'full moon' joke the staff member shared that night and found a pen, under the radiator, that the emergency room physician had lost in all the hub bub, they went wild! The staff were amazed by my story but perhaps even more so, by the fact that I made a full comeback.

I now know fully, from the deepest part of my being, that death does not exist."

My friend's story transformed a simple campfire into a magical
life teaching, one that has inspired my entire life.
The key was in the two questions...
"What did you learn?" and "Whom did you help?"

So accordingly,
The Prime Directive,
The reason you are here, is...

To grow in every way, and
To uplift, inspire, and help, wherever you may go or be sent.

To GROW and TO SERVE

COMMANDMENT 1

Thou shalt grow (evolve yourself) in every way possible.

"He who is not busy being born, is busy dying."
Bob Dylan

After a lifetime of helping people prepare for their final parting journey, here is what has become clear and obvious.

· The folks who are best prepared to die are the ones who have done the most work on themselves and for others.

You know this.
Here's some other things you may or may not remember.

· Earth existence is a necessary course of study for our soul's evolution and eventual liberation.

· You voluntarily chose to come to Earth.

· You not only volunteered, but your immortal soul, along with the wisdom of your spiritual guides, worked out a game plan.

· The game plan you designed is a spiritual blueprint, a life template, like a vision statement for your soul's journey here. This map holds the momentum for circumstances of your life to unfold. Essentially, before we take on existence, we choose the basic premises for this life's needed based on the karmic history of our soul's journey. We choose our families, our goals, and the major lessons we need to experience on Earth. All this is intelligently worked out based on what is needed for your specific growth.

All for you.

This concept of the *"sacred blueprint"* is our soul's DNA pattern for this life. Problem is, as soon as we embody, it is as if our memory has been erased. Like a fresh start, for a new lease on your present soul's existence. That tabla rasa, blank slate thing. It does not matter if you believe in an eternally growing soul.
Or a past life. Or a new incarnation. Or any of this.

1

It makes no difference what you believe.

What is going to happen to you, happens.

How you respond to life's lessons, whether you learn and grow from the lessons or play victim, is what counts.

Whether you realize it or not, by coming down to Earth, you have enrolled yourself into this **Grand School of Evolution.** But once here, you are kind of on your own recognizance and the circumstances can change by your own free will.

Here is the difficult part to wrap your head around, this is an Interactive Universe. It is here, in this land filled with intense feelings and emotions, that we get direct lessons and evolve the quickest. It is here that every lesson is your lesson, created specifically for you to learn. Sounds wild and far-fetched, it is not, and the clock is running, so let's get with the program. As Ram Dass says, *"It's the only dance there is."*

Like any school, everyone is at a different level of growth and understanding. Some are beginners, others advanced, old souls. Because you've showed an interest by reading this book, you are probably the latter.

No worries. Though, if you are down here, regardless of your grade level, you still are in a place of little brainers. Our world, your world, is also a combination of these levels, and please remember what the Master says, *"In my Father's house, there are many mansions."*

THE ELEMENTARY SCHOOL LEVEL OF CONSCIOUSNESS

The Elementary school level of consciousness is where we start. It's our root grounding. Living in this consciousness is that of survival and the fulfillment of basic needs: food, shelter, safety. When growing up, if your parents or caregivers consistently met your needs, your world felt secure. But that is not a given and many people the world over live in an unstable and insecure environment. It can be a worldly mentality, base, very often vulgar, even animalistic.

This survival mode is not that dissimilar to Darwin's "Survival of the fittest."

The notion," It's a jungle out there," is the very epitome of living to meet basic needs.

Survival, security issues; the Elementary level is the foundation that many humans live with and dwell in.

Sometimes survival is all they know, a mere step up the evolutionary ladder from our canine and mammalian friends.

This population often makes up the most violent and self-absorbed in our society.

Crack, heroin, murder, deceit, thievery, even genocide, all have their origins in the fear and insecurity of new souls grappling with and living at this primitive or basic level of consciousness. It doesn't necessarily have to be a dog-eat-dog level and thankfully, very often it isn't. We have all originally come from here. In Abraham Maslow's Hierarchy of Needs, these folks are on the first rung of his ladder of evolution, the neediest.

This level's mantra is, "What's in it for me?"

"When we are afraid of ourselves and afraid of the seeming threat the world presents then we become extremely selfish. We build our own little nests, cocoons to live securely."
Chogyam Trungpa Rinpoche

THE JUNIOR HIGH LEVEL OF CONSCIOUSNESS

The Junior High-level folks are the people that work their daily 9 to 5, come home, eat dinner, and enjoy a bowl of ice cream as they watch Matlock on television. They could easily be the neighborhood, even the family you grew up in. They possess and quite often nurture tribal prejudices and loyalties. Racism and intolerance can dwell and prosper at this level. Junior high-level folks do little self-inquiry as to the purpose of their existence or the many other spiritual considerations of life. These individuals are very often the hard working "schlubs" of our society or more respectfully, the "Salt of the Earth."

This level's mantra is, *"There's a sale at Macy's".*

THE HIGH SCHOOL LEVEL OF CONSCIOUSNESS

At this level of consciousness, we begin to see questioning as to the purpose of life. Why am I here, what is all this craziness about?

Like itching powder under our spiritual skin, humans' quest to understand, to evolve.

It's in your DNA to grow.

So, in turn, it is common to seek out individuals or long-term traditions that appear to know the purpose of life or have answers.

That's what religion is all about for many people. From EST training to Swami Mama lama dingdong, high school level folks become born again anything if their adopted persuasion has a semblance of an answer to the questions. Even when this answer smacks of inconsistencies or clear hypocrisies, they are kept in the fold by their tribal elders with the faith card. *"You must have faith; all your questions will be answered in the by and by."*

The new programming comes complete with a pledge of allegiance and a temporary identity card. Fill in your new label, "Hi, I'm Larry, I am a born-again Zoroastrian". This allows us to hold onto some seemingly solid reality in a world that is increasingly frightening, unstable, and threatening to our security (ego). And it is precisely these labels that create the separation and division in our world. Whether it's genuine, intellectual sloth or tunnel-blind comfortable, your newfound security only lasts while you are not paying attention to your insomnia or the folds of fat developing around your waist. And you know gaining weight is one of the sure-fire ways to tell that you are not paying attention or addressing something important.

This level's mantra is *"I believe, I believe, I believe, I really do".*

THE COLLEGE LEVEL

At this level, you become acutely aware of existential anxiety, the apprehension surrounding the question,

"What is the purpose of life?" and perhaps more poignantly, . . "What is the purpose of my life?"

To sate or sedate the emptiness and pain of not fulfilling our destiny, we try to fill ourselves in from the outside. That's why most humans are driven to self-medicate in some fashion, if only to make themselves feel a little better for a short while.

Filling yourself up even temporarily to drown out the noise screaming in your head is quite often the path many take.

There are many detours that quell the unfulfillment: food, sugar, drugs, alcohol, gambling, sex, possessions, constant entertainment, power trips, even fame and riches. All to keep quiet and sometimes numb for a time.

Unfortunately, "more detours" eventually wears thin and our hunger returns in some way to remind us we are not fulfilling our destiny.

Incidentally, your emptiness does not go away even when you become a famous household name or possess all the earth's riches.

Remember what we said, filling yourself in from the outside does not fulfill your heart's longing; it just takes your attention off the spiritual barrenness of your life, and temporarily at that. Can you say, "spiritual detour"?

This level's mantra is, "How shall we entertain ourselves tonight?"

THE MASTERS LEVEL

The Bible states, *"Seek ye first the kingdom of heaven and all else shall be prepared unto thee."*

Simply put, work on yourself first and everything else you do will likewise improve.

Whether it is your relationships, your art, your music, your work, or your play, when you strive to grow by improving yourself, by striving to be your very finest, empowerment and especially contentment eventually follows.

When you consistently do not live up to your higher self, life can become meaningless, and death often frightening. How many of us had dreams of doing something special with our life? Making a difference. A contribution to touch the world in some way.

Perhaps you did not learn the tools to live up to fulfilling your life's mission, your sacred contract.

By going inside, by sincerely working on ourselves, we begin to connect to our higher self, our destiny. This interior decorating is a full spectrum job, encompassing our body, mind, emotions, and spirit. When you begin to undertake this overhaul, you will begin to get happy. After a bunch of years at this growth, evolution, and excellence thing, you are no longer just Larry from Denville; you are becoming St. Larry from Denville. Your life will be a continuous teaching, a spiritual adventure movie. Every experience and every person will be part of the sets and cast. You are the producer, director, writer, and main actor.

People who have the courage and iron-clad will to lead a committed life are truly blessed.

Their aging is not filled with fear, regrets, or trepidation of the unknown.

As they age, they fully come into their power and wisdom. So will you.

Take your choice of master souls: Jesus, Buddha, Lao Tzu, Ramana Maharshi, St. Theresa.

As they continued their intense daily spiritual work (sadhana), they discovered their internal lightning rod, their connection to the Great Spirit, the Father, the Tao.

AND SO WILL YOU!

THE DOCTORAL LEVEL

The doctoral-level individuals have already graduated to the next level of consciousness (post-doctoral, the next world). They come down here to make a difference. Like a shift in the force.

These great souls give up the heaven world they earned through lifetimes of courage, diligence, and spiritual perseverance and make a return engagement to help us blokes down here.

Remember, there would be no prospectors if there wasn't gold in them, there hills.

Just be certain it isn't fool's gold.

Like my brother Richard says,

"The spirit is here for all to share, it's in your hair, in the air, and it can't be bought, sold, bargained for wholesale or retail."

"I am here to tell you, you are perfect, worthy instruments of God. If there is to be a future on this planet, it will rest in the hands of those who have the courage to make a stand for truth, for the children. From this day on, believe you are the district representative and spokesperson for the Holy Spirit. You are the sons and daughters of God, believe it, act like it, you got connections!"

So, let's do a quick review on what is necessary for you to fulfill Commandment One.

Your life condition and how you express yourself physically, mentally, even psychologically as a human is the sum total of your genetics, your conditioning, your nutritional intake and the environment you live in along with how you live your life.

PHYSICALLY
The Short version

It's about how and what you eat, the supporting supplements you take, the water you drink, the cosmetics you use and the exercise that shapes your body and energetic vision. I guess I'm saying, how you live in your world. It's how we break up our body's stagnation and hardness.

For starters...

EAT MORE LIKE JESUS

History records Jesus as a pescatarian (plant-based diet with small amounts of supplemental fish).

But now things have changed dramatically since Jesus. Now it's time to eat organic plant-based food, drink alkaline water, and use organic products for your cosmetic and cleaning needs.

When you can, just STOP eating animals.

It shortens your life.

Take a good supplement program rich in essential fatty acids, vitamin D, lots of antioxidants, green tea, etc. Laboratory animals live much longer when given antioxidants. I believe folks that take supplements live longer, too.

Do a varied, inspiring exercise routine, work hard, get and keep flexible, keep your spine open. You don't have to wear yourself out or use yourself up to be fit. Be aware of your inflammatory condition.

So many great ways to get physical.

If there is a rule, it might be this:

Folks that stand live longer than folks that sit, and folks that move live longer than both.

Ok, that's the short version.

There is lots of nutrition information later in this book.

EMOTIONALLY
The Short version

It's learning how not to give your power away by playing the victim.

Nobody can make you feel bad without your permission.

Stop giving away your power.

Learn how to act, not react.

It's learning how to hold center in an authentic, empathic way. There's an amazing chapter on working emotionally later in this book.

MENTALLY
The Short version

It's training your mind to have pinpoint focus and then how to empty it and make it still like a crystal-clear lake with no ripples.

SPIRITUALLY
The Short version

This work is about doing street time, essentially helping out, working to improve and uplift the world around you.

SUM TOTAL

It's going to take real consistency, commitment, and sometimes bulldog determination.

Start by doing one thing at a time: one day, one assignment, one goal.

A spiritual life is a daily grind.

You grind up your ego and make yourself invisible, like the Holy Spirit.

Then you'll become a force to be reckoned with.

Like the St. Francis song written by Donovan:
"If you want your dream to be, build it slow and surely.
Small beginnings greater ends. Heartfelt work grows purely.
If you want to live life free,
Take your time go slowly.
Do few things but do them well,
Simple joys are holy.
Day by day, stone by stone,
Build your secret slowly.
Day by day, you'll grow, too,
You'll know heaven's glory."
"You must possess a warrior spirit, to have the courage to face your naked truth."

COMMANDMENT 2

Thou Shalt HELP...
serve, uplift and inspire one another,
wherever you may go, wherever you are sent.

"Thou shalt be a mandala to each other"
Rich rishi Heisler

Reading from the King James Version, Book of Mark, Chapter Ten, and Verses 35 through 45, we discover that Jesus' disciples James and John have a request for the master.

35 "Master," they said, "we would that thou shouldest do for us whatsoever we shall desire."

36 "And he said unto them, what would ye that I should do for you?"

37 "They said unto him, Grant unto us that we may sit, one at thy right hand, and the other on thy left hand, in thy glory."
And Jesus said,

40 "But to sit at my right hand and my left hand is not mine to give; but it shall be given to them for whom it is prepared."

43 "But so shall it not be among you: but whosoever will be great among you, shall be your servant."

44 "And whosoever of you will be the chiefest, shall be servant of all."

Now to really fulfill this commandment;
to help, serve, uplift and inspire one another,
wherever you may go;
you will need to know the following.

There are both light and dark forces on this planet. Taoist cosmology says, from the one Great Spirit, come the two opposing forces, yin and yang, male and female. Successful life on this planet is a balancing of these two opposing forces, what the Taoists call yin and yang. Jesus supports this concept when he talks about alpha and omega, when he says, my father is a motion and a rest and especially when he says, **when you learn to balance your left hand from your right, your right hand from your left, the kingdom of heaven shall be open unto you.**

Before we embrace the Prime Directive, before we even know our purpose in life, we are basically unimportant to the great scheme of things. To simplify, I'm going to make up another word, shmendricks. Simple shmendricks, we can disappear in this great stew of life, left somewhat on our own recognizance.

As long as we continue to have nothing really outstanding to contribute, meandering from one neurotic addiction/detour to another, this formula can basically stand pat.

However, the moment we decide to **embrace the prime directive,** that is *"to grow,"* everything changes!

Physics tells us that "Every action has an equal and opposite reaction". When you live in Spirit and inspire those around you to evolve, you become a danger to the forces of entropy, to the dark side.

Suddenly, you are working on yourself. The greater your commitment to personal transformation, the more likely you are to create a remarkable shift in your life. Not only are you becoming more and more extraordinary, this evolutionary transformation in you will influence the lives of everyone around you. Profound!

Everyone the Universe sends your way.

Remember...interactive Universe. Alive with consciousness. During your life, you will touch the lives of thousands, perhaps even millions of people. With all this growth, you are now a threat to the stability (chaos) of the planet.

That's right, CHAOS has been woven into the fabric of our beloved Earth. Yin and yang going back to the One. That's our goal. Back to the One perfection.

If you are fulfilling your DNA's natural destiny to evolve, you have chosen sides. Remember, Mahatma Ghandi was virtually unknown before the age of sixty.

WARNING: Be ever so vigilant because the dark side is much more sophisticated than you can imagine. It is fueled by the earth's natural order, and it can lurk in the shadows of your lower self. It can come up with ways to throw you off your spiritual path that are brilliant and personally devastating to you. Remember, there is no good or bad in this, just opposing forces performing their endless dance of life on this planetary level. It is the way this place has been set up. Do not gripe. You will go beyond it, in time.

There are three main ways that the dark side will try and keep you from coming into your power:

1. It will bring up your old, neurotic tapes and inequities, the circumstances that have pressed your buttons since you were a youngster. These button-pressing annoyances can include fears, insecurities, jealousies, impatience, your weight, the size of your body parts, your hair, the size of your nose or butt; all in all, your immature ego junk. The dark side will find ways to mess with you, endlessly keeping you on the treadmill of reacting to this stuff. Like a bad dream, you will be on a permanent detour, a victim of your mind. That is, <u>until you stop feeding it</u>. And when that happens, you will move on and lose interest in fueling and supporting your lower ego junk.

2. The temptations of life can be very attractive. Money, power, security, companionship, status, are very alluring and very intoxicating. After you have made the decision to grow, that is when the fun begins. The tests will come when you least expect them. From left field or right in your own circle. Do you remember what Al Pacino says as he plays the devil in the movie "Devil's Advocate"? *"I'm the hand up Mona Lisa's dress, they never see me coming."* Imagine you're eating really well for perhaps the first time, or the first time in a while.

You are meditating regularly, staying optimistic, exercising, taking your vitamins consistently, studying, really getting your life together. Then, "poof", you show up on the dark side's radar and suddenly, you get this great job offer, or the seemingly perfect man or woman comes into your life, or the investment of a lifetime becomes available or _____ fill in the blank).

All the dark side needs to do is give you a detour. If we can be detoured at critical times in our life, our life can amount to nothing much really. Most people go from one detour to another and at the end of their life, you hear them exclaim, *"I had so many dreams, so many opportunities, I don't know where the time has gone"*.

The clearer you are, the more deeply the people you meet will be transformed. Sometimes, all it will take is a word. It has to be the exact right word at that exact right time. If you met a saint in the elevator, what would that saint say? If they read you spiritually, the magic of that moment could plant the seed to change your entire life. So now, imagine yourself as that saint. You must be so empty of yourself that you can discern and intuit what that word or phrase is for a person you've never met. There are only a limited number of people you can touch in the course of your life. Get out there, the clock is ticking.

Just remember Jesus out in the desert. He drew a sacred circle around himself for protection. When the devil came and did his best to lure the master over to the dark side Jesus was more than capable of resisting. **Be on the lookout for the detours, pay attention** and use a jaundiced eye.

3. Sometimes you can lead an impeccable life with little karmic mistakes and stuff still happens. You know, "only the good die young" idea. The last way the dark side can detour your life's vision is really not the dark side's own creation. We might define it as the negative power influencing our life, but really, it's of our own creation.

In our soul's evolution, in our past lives, we have done things that are less than admirable.

Haven't you complained about Murphy's Law (everything that can go wrong, will go wrong) sometime in your life? There have certainly been times in my life where it has seemed all too much.

Ram Dass use to say, *"It's not too much, it's just enough."* I also heard him say, and this is from an in-class memory so I'm paraphrasing, *"Thank you God for putting me through such crap"*. It's through the fire that we can be cleansed. Chalk it up to all those misspent past lives.

Since we reap what we sow and in the grand scheme of things there is no timeline, it's quite possible that your suffering today is a product of some long past one comeuppance.

Maybe you come from a family of slave traders, butchers, or warriors. Maybe you were in the Crusades or killed in self-defense. Who knows?

We have all witnessed wonderful people suffering terribly for no apparent reason.

As I said before, the only way to circumvent the unknown payoff's from coming our way is through service.

Service to humankind is like working off a bad debt.

You can lessen your karma's severity by *consistently thinking outward with an open heart.* That's why they call it "karma yoga", the yoga of service.

If you were to die right this very instant, what would your eulogy sound like? *"He was a wonderful man/woman, a devoted father/mother and friend. Remember the year he donated money to the United Way and when he helped out for the school play?"* When eulogizing a deceased loved one, it's natural for a minister to be generous with praise and accolades. At my own father's funeral, the eulogy made him almost unrecognizable. It was, however, very consoling for my mother.

Have you ever been to a funeral service where the deceased wasn't one of the greatest people that ever lived?

Florinda Donner-Grau is one of Carlos Castenanda's teachers. Castenanda was a very successful author and spiritual teacher in the 20th century. His remarkable books outlined the mystical ways of the shamans he explored and studied with. In a wonderful interview written by Michael Brennan and published in the Utne Reader, Florinda says, *"Death is your truest friend, and your most reliable adviser. If you ever have doubts about the course of your life, you have only to consult your death for proper direction. Death will never lie to you."*

Wouldn't it be cool if the minister at your own funeral could say with total honesty that you lived an impeccable life? That in that life, you had made a personal stand for truth, for people and for children. That you touched people's hearts with your warmth and your humor, but most importantly, with your **love**. It was the amazing quality of your love that inspired us to be better people ourselves.

Your life improved the quality of our lives and that made a powerful difference in our world.

Why couldn't this be your eulogy?

Jesus said, *"Be transformed by the renewing of your mind...".* What if we take him up on that?

So, this moment, this very instant..., while you are reading these words, what if from this moment on, you try to live an impeccable life.

You clean up things in a big way.

Somehow, you find the courage and the grit to fully **believe in yourself.**

Believe that this is what your life can be about.

Walking the walk.

Know it!

You can fulfill your destiny.

You CAN be a hero.

Hilda called this an *"immediate adjustment of mind."*

You've also heard it called *"an instant shock of God awakening"*!

That moment when your little self has been moved out and you're plugged into your Higher Self, your "I and my Father are one" self.

Yeah, that kind of plugged in.

It's not just words.

"You are a light unto the world."

Ya gotta Believe it!

Live today as if it were your last day on Earth.

Now, go out and be a light unto the world.

Start doing that every day and you'll make a profound difference in the great scheme of things.

"Far greater things, you shall do, than I have done."

It's time to begin a dialogue with yourself. To push yourself to become most extraordinary, you have to prime the divine pump in yourself to bring out your own mojo.

Don't you remember the revelation in church John Belushi had in the movie The Blues Brothers? He heard from on high.... he was on a **mission from God!**

Aren't we all on a mission?

There was a great Cuban shaman (Santeria) in Jersey City named Orestes. Orestes devoted his life to practicing the healing art of spiritual medicine. He would invoke the healing powers and direct them to purge his patients of their afflictions. He was real, he was spiritually beautiful, and he was ever powerful. On Mondays Orestes would invite selected people from Hilda's group to his studio. It was there he would teach and transform the room into a spiritual vortex for healing. And like a coach, he made you believe in your innate ability to feel, to intuit, and to develop your inner sight.

He would scream at YOU...

"OPEN YOUR EYES!
WHAT DO YOU SEE?"

Orestes didn't really care if you saw the person's aura or energy field. He was trying to get you to see beyond the limitation of your mind, so he would keep banging at you in an overwhelming way until you had a breakthrough.

You could have said anything, *"I see orange or a rainbow"*. It didn't make a difference as long as you were attempting to project your inner sight. Then with the healing portion, he would continue:

"Open your heart energy... Now send your healing LOVE,
Go beyond your little self... use your God-given gifts! USE YOUR
GIFTS!"

After two hours of banging down your own ego, week after week of pushing yourself beyond your spiritual limits, your inner voice and sight gradually awakened and new healing sensibilities took hold.

Orestes gave birth to some wonderful healers that have devoted their lives to doing good. A great legacy for any teacher. The point is, to fulfill the prime directive and live up those powerful words, you are going to need to talk to yourself, to psyche yourself daily with a tremendous optimism. You literally have to step up as if you were a great spiritual athlete.

There is, however, one thing that you can do to top the original great eulogy. Perhaps the only life-path more profoundly graced than expressed before. Live up to all those amazing words and do it anonymously. You heard me right. Leave no trail, particularly if your life really changed the world. In Carlos

Castaneda books, he introduces us to his teacher, a master shaman called Don Juan. Don Juan taught Carlos Castaneda, *"It is imperative to leave aside what is called personal history."* In a divine state the "me", as in personal importance, just doesn't count.

My personal journey has taken me to work with many people during the dying stages of life. The individuals that embraced this concept of serving, uplifting, and inspiring, were more often than not blessed. They were also not as afraid of dying. In fact, they were very much at peace.

The only thing you can bring with you to the other side, at the end of your life, is the growth you have acquired and the good you have done.

ALSO, more selfishly and a very wise word, to the wise... one of the only ways I know to circumvent life's travails, the karma coming due your way, is by making a powerful difference.

If what you reap is what you sow, and every action has an equal and opposite reaction, then be first in excellence, be first in love and be first in service. Use your every waking moment to inspire your brothers and sisters into awake-ness and establish yourself as a center of peace and unconditional love.

"The love you take is equal to the love you make." The Beatles

COMMANDMENT 3

Thou Shalt Be a Co-Creator

*"Pray as if everything depended on God
and work as if everything depended on you."*
Cardinal Spellman

My father-in-law visited me in a dream nine months after he passed over to the other side. It turned out to be a dream with a *"wakeup call"* life message.

At that time, I was trying to live a spiritually committed life. Plenty of meditation, trying to chew each mouthful of brown rice until it turned to liquid and practicing yoga, breath, and chi healing arts daily. I would travel into the city three times a week for Hilda's extraordinary meditation class. Hilda taught her students to have a spiritual hunger. She believed it was better to be *"Hellbent for Heaven"* then to be weak and indecisive about spiritual practice. She was fond of reminding us that *"God spews out of his mouth the lukewarm."*

Yeah, she could be intense.

That is why she was so fantastic and touched so many lives!

OK. Back to my father-in-law visiting me in a dream nine months after he passed on.

Here's how the dream unfolded.

"Hi Dad," I exclaimed, filled with excitement, *"I've been waiting for you to visit me".*

Smiling with his deep, natural warmth and wisdom, the first words from my father-in-law's mouth were,

"Let's take a walk," he said nonchalantly. *"Would you like to get something to eat?"* he continued.

"They have restaurants on this side, Dad?" I questioned, fumbling with my words and delightful amazement.

"No" ... he said,

"On this side, it is a mental world.

You visualize what you would like, hold its image firmly in your mind's eye and breathe your power into that image." ....

"What would you like to have?" Dad pressed.

"I would like..., how about, a slice of whole wheat pizza?"
At that moment Dad instructed,
"Ok, stand firm, pull in, take a deep breath, clear your brain, now strongly visualize all the atoms of that slice coming together, the cheese..., the sauce..., the crust..., the plate...."
As I followed his directions, in front of my eyes, a seeming mass of colors and textures appeared to be forming.
As if being pulled from the fabric of space itself, its atoms binding in the creation of the perfect slice.
Then suddenly, something caught my attention at the side of my mind's eye.
It could not have been more than a split second when my attention shifted.
And poof.........., the entire mass I was creating with my now momentarily jaded concentration plummeted to the ground in a heaping mass of confusion and atomic disunity.
My father-in-law looked me straight in the eye and simply said, *"Your vision is not yet clear enough"* and dissolved in the ether.
That was the last time I saw him. But now I feel him all the time.

The term "co-creation" has been bandied about in many of the world's religious traditions and scripture. From Jesus' line, *"I and my father are one",* to repeating the Hindu prayer line, *"Om Tat Sat Tat Sat Om",* meaning, *"I am that I am".* One of the most inspirational of explanations about co-creation comes from Barbara Marx Hubbard. Barbara is the world-renowned futurist and seer that noble prize laureate R. Buckminster Fuller said, *"Is the best-informed human alive regarding futurism".*
Barbara's contention is that we are on the threshold of a new human species. We are evolving and giving birth to a new state of consciousness that she calls, *"empathetic attunement to the voice within".* Using Jesus as our model for the *"future human,"* we are ready to share the responsibility of planetary growth, development, and management with our higher mind or *"God-mind".*

Michio Kushi, the man who promoted his amazing macrobiotic diet to combat disease worldwide, explains it something like this; when we are in our mother's womb we live in a world of darkness. An ocean-like environment provides the backdrop for our 270-day trek to the next level of evolution, our birth. Our placenta in the womb partially protects us from the outside elements. If life favors us, we can successfully be birthed into this new, next world.

Instead of darkness, there is darkness and light, instead of the fluid world of the placenta, there is now air. Michio compares our trek in the womb to the first crustaceans leaving the great oceans to become air breathers on the shoreline. Likewise, we go from a water world inside mom to an air world when birthed.

Now you and I are protected by a sort of placenta we call our body.

We are also in preparation for the next level of evolution, but this time it might take 70, 80 or even 90 years.

We're talking about life expectancy. This time our next destination is my father-in-law's world of Light on the other side.

The world of vibrational energy. And like my father-in-law illustrated, that world is directly influenced by the power of your mind.

This next world of Light and mind make this world look infantile, like a beginner's program.

Kushi calls this evolutionary trek from single-celled existence in our mother's womb, through our life in the human world and then into this new world of incorporeal consciousness, *"FROM DARKNESS UNTO LIGHT."*

In early religious training, this journey was referred to as the *"Great Chain of Being"*.

From mineral to plant, from plant to animal, from animal to human, from human to angelic, and from angelic back to the one supreme consciousness, God.

The Great Chain of Being was a sort of reference chart for our soul's continuing development. In a sense, it earmarked the levels of spiritual evolution.

Our world has been referred to as a planet of *"little brainers"*. Hindu scripture refers to this time as the Kali Yuga, or the *"Iron Age"*. In truth, we have been living in an age of virtual ignorance.

However, we're at the very end of that time and we are entering into a dramatically new and liberating moment.

So, our planet Earth turns out to be an evolutionary cooker of consciousness from animals evolving to humans and humans developing to the next level of frequency, angelic (light body). I have heard it said that humans use only six percent of their brains' capacity while a pig uses a mere four percent. Only two percent smarter than a pig, huh? Now that's a humbling thought. It's not surprising then that we spray our agricultural crops with toxic, carcinogenic chemicals and in turn feed them to our children. It is hard to develop a big ego when you think about it in that way. To be a co-creator in the Casa Loca, this crazy house we call Earth, can seem like a momentous job. So here we are on this ass backward planet, gathering our lessons of growth to graduate to the next level.

By recognizing your relationship with the universal power, higher self or the divine, co-creation provides the tools toward transformation. One can utilize visualization, prayer, programming, or positive affirmation. As in believing the force is with you and a part of your genetic inheritance. The Essenes referred to their disciples as the "sons of God" and the "daughters of God". Pretty powerful family you come from. *"Those that have a vision for the future, have a future filled with vision".*

So, to get on with this co-creation stuff, **you will need to open up your energetic system.** Raise your vibratory rate, so to speak. Any spiritualizing techniques or exercises will do. The list could include dancing, stretching, playing music, breathing exercises, candle gazing, Do-In (self-acupressure massage), gardening, painting, composing, mantra, chanting, chi kung, yoga, sun salutations, especially deep tissue massage therapy, and of course lots of prayer and meditation., More is better. By priming the pump of your spiritual reservoir, by raising your Soul frequency, you will have an abundance of charge (chi) to use for your vision. Find the things you like that give you real juice. It might be a personal inspiration.

Next, you must train your mind to focus powerfully and pointedly. That is where intensity, patience, breathing and practice defragment your brain. In time, you will be able to set your intention in your mind's eye and send out a continuous wave force. It is this type of continued practice that will help manifest your dreams, aspirations and prayers. Thinking is to your intentions as watering is to plants.

Hilda used to tell us to keep a notebook for our prayers and intentions. After our meditation, she wanted us to take out our book and reaffirm our requests. She called it the Power of Scientific Prayer. Whether that be prayers for people struggling with issues and illnesses or special requests for our family's needs.

She would say, *"The only way God can have a clear picture of what you want, kids, is to put your order in by writing it down."*

Remember the guy or gal you so vehemently desired to date in high school? You know, the one that didn't even know you existed back then?

This was before you trained your mind with meditation. Well, your thoughts about that person were registered in the great physics of our universe. Now, twenty-five years later, you go to your high school reunion. And there he or she is not only recognizing you but ready, willing, and available. But now, she/he is not quite as attractive as you remembered. In fact, they aged rather poorly and you're questioning yourself, "What was I thinking?" It took twenty-five years for your focused attention (prayer) to come around to fruition.

The secret formula to activate Newton's Third Law of Motion, **"Every action has an equal and opposite reaction,"** is a **vociferously trained mind and will.**

The more you pray and meditate, the more quickly your intention will come to pass. Even down here it is a mental universe, every thought has a power behind it. The more power behind your thoughts, the more quickly they will manifest. Thus you are an active participant in co-creation.

One Friday evening, I arrived late for Hilda's advanced class. I must have looked somewhat disheveled.

Hilda glanced my way and said, *"What's going on with you, kid?"*

"Well Hilda," I sheepishly said, *"I spent the day with the realtor looking for a house."*

"Did you write down exactly what you want in your intention notebook?"

"No Hilda".
"How many times must I remind you kids how to use God's power? she scolded.
"You probably missed out on the precise house you wanted by not using your power; write down what it is you want!"
That next day I gave my realtor a detailed description of what we really wanted. My note to the realtor said, *"A blue house, with central air conditioning and wall-to wall-carpeting. On or across from Lake Musconetcong, with an acre of property that is flat and easy to manage and all for $85,000 dollars."*
My realtor laughed and said facetiously, *"Is that all you want?"*
Not two days later, he called and said, *"I can't believe it! I found your exact house and it's on the street named after you—Lawrence Avenue."* The blue house was across from the lake with all the accoutrements requested and it was magnificent. We immediately drove over and put down a deposit.

Only to find it was sold four hours prior to our getting there. When I told Hilda, she busted up in laughter.
"Good lesson, huh kid?"
This is an interactive Universe, the clearer your intention, the more luminous and powerful your vibration, the quicker you will reap what you sow. Have big dreams!

At the beginning of Hilda's class, she would start with a centering meditation. Standing at attention with our hands behind our back as if we were on the bridge of the starship Enterprise, she would have us close our eyes and visualize. Her words were concise and forceful.

"Stand firm, kids. Pull in; get strong. Envision from the top of your head to the tip of your toes a wave of golden Light.
Every cell, every atom of your body is endowed with this Light.
Now, as if there was a nose in the center of your chest, breathe into your heart center.
Breathe love in and breathe it to every cell of your body.
Breathe love in and breathe it out to the world.
Feel as if all your bodies are aligning physical body, firm and flexible; emotional body, calm and smooth; mental body, right here, right now. Open your spine and raise your spiritual energy to the top of your head. This moment will never come again, kids; experience it fully."
Hilda would then have us open our eyes.
With our right hand in front of our face (thumb on our nose and

forefinger at the height of our third eye), she would exclaim, "Now kids, pull your hand down the center of your body and as you pull it down, feel your physical body aligning and getting firm. Now pull your hand down again; this time feel your emotions and mind get calm and completely one-pointed. Now fill your entire aura with golden healing Light." "This", she would say, "is the way you should live. Body, mind, emotions centered and in alignment. When all of your bodies are aligned, God can work through you and make a miracle."

After years of spiritual inner work, I have seen the spirit work through me in amazing and powerful ways. On a daily basis, synchronicity happens.

In the mid-1980s, I was looking for a home in the lake region of New Jersey. My best friend, family physician and environmental activist Dr. Wally, insisted that before I purchase anything, I must learn about radon gas and its insipid dangers.

Just for the record, I had never heard of radon gas.

He continued by explaining that his very good friend was one of the foremost radiation experts in the country. Aside from being asked to offer scientific testimony on a regular basis in Washington D.C., this friend had recently been called in to consult for the State of New Jersey. Apparently, New Jersey was/ is considered a "hot" state, rich in uranium, playing host to a highly carcinogenic gas leaking up from the ground called *radon*. It would seep into the basements of homes invisible and undetected. Radon was estimated to cause, 33,000 lung cancer deaths per year in NJ alone. Dr. Wally also had a friend who was a geologist and former Department of Environmental Protection (DEP) employee. This friend got into medical school with Dr. Wally's help, so Dr. Wally decided to call in a favor. One phone call and the geologist and I had an appointment to meet with the resident radon expert at the Department of Environmental Protection in Trenton. We were cordially greeted and invited into her office. We put our notepads and materials on her desk and began to fire off our questions and concerns. She began by saying that we had nothing to be concerned about. Radon was essentially a non-issue and should not be a determining factor in the purchase of a home. We went into an adjoining room where she showed us some aerial topographical maps of the hot spots in question. We asked how we can get copies of these maps. She said there is an office that sells them but added they probably don't have them, and they are quite expensive. With that we followed her back to her desk and essentially, she sent us on our way. I picked up our materials from her desk, thanked her for her time and left. On the way home, we did stop at the state map department and purchased what was to be their last set of maps. When we arrived back at my office, I thanked Dr. Wally's friend for accompanying me and handed him what I thought was his file. He simply said "Oh, that must be yours", shook my hand and left. When I opened the mysterious file, the first page was stamped CONFIDENTIAL. The file contained a slew of letters, documents, and research data from the Department of Environmental Protection to the Governor's office and back. The data therein confirmed exactly what Wally had reported to me. There are an estimated thirty-three thousand cancer deaths a year due to radon exposure and very few people know about it. I do not know how long the information was available or if it was really suppressed or why. Realizing that I inadvertently picked up the file accidentally, I called our doctor at the DEP and told her of my discovery. She vehemently requested that I send the file back Overnight Express, which I did. But not before I made a complete copy and called my friend Dr. Wally. Wally was one of the most famous environmentalists in the Northeast. In fact, during the 1980s Ralph Nader exclaimed that Wally's nonprofit organization entitled "Food and Water" was the most effective environmental organization in the United States. With Wally's connections, the next day the front pages of the Daily Record and the Star Ledger were filled with the cancer death details. Imagine...33,000 lung cancer deaths per year and no one in government thought it would be important enough to make public! Moreover, I had the maps, which turned out to show much more than just the hot spots. My one-bedroom garden apartment became overrun with reporters, photographers, and interested parties. There were maps spread out over our tables and floors. For at least a week, it looked like a mob scene.

All of this happened by a simple quirk of fate.

I had no espionage in mind when I went to Trenton; it was just dumb coincidence. In a short period of time legislation was passed and laws were put into effect regarding the sale of homes and the deadly radon gases. Folks learned how to mitigate the poison gas. Many people who might have suffered terribly were thankfully spared. A total fluke.
If you believe in flukes.

Dr. Wally Burnstein, the founder of Food and Water, organized against the irradiation of food.

When asked by polluters to compromise, he responded, *"OK, let's compromise. Who gets cancer—my child or yours?"*

What you must appreciate is that I have spent my whole life trying to teach about health and wellness.

I was Director of Nutrition for a medical facility, had given hundreds of nutrition workshops to literally thousands of people, and along with my wife ran a natural food cooking school for individuals with degenerative illness. And yet, when it came to touching people's lives, this was perhaps the single greatest thing I had ever done. I was in the right place at the right time and made the right phone call to the right person.

I still scratch my head when I think about it.

The lesson I received was this:

If you are to be used by Spirit in the co-creative process, you must be ready, by continually working on yourself, holding center and paying attention to the omens all around you. You never know when you'll be called upon.

I fully expect amazing things to happen every day, and they do.

Recap: You have been banished to the planet of the "little brainers."

You are older souls, but before you can go about your Father's work, you must first come into your power.

When your foundation is strong and disciplined, when you realize that your training is in your day-to-day actions and surroundings, then your work will be planetary.

You will have graduated to become an emissary of the Light workers.

You will be given a territory and assignments.

You will be a conduit and spokesperson for all that is good, loving, and light. When your foundation is thus, you cannot be moved, possessed, or victimized.

This is a literal Universe.

Be very clear about what you ask for.

Many years ago, my students were very intent on me writing this book. I even had a publisher coming to my meditation classes and exhorting me to write this book.

I was taking the family on holiday to Disney. I thought it would be a good time to begin creating the outline.

I was so busy putting everything in order to go on the vacation with two little kids that I asked everyone around me if they passed a store that sold Sony Walkman's to pick one up for me. I figured I could talk into the recorder and begin an outline for my book. Alas, none of us had the time to purchase one for our trip, so I had to forego it. The last day at Disney I got to see how closely the Universe was listening. We went to MGM Studios. After running around much of the damp and hot Florida day with two little children on day five of our Disney vacation, we decided it might be good to take a rest in an air-conditioned auditorium. Soon, we found ourselves in a line to be part of the new television game show offering of The Price Is Right. We were the very last ones in the line to be granted admission, which was simply great!

We found ourselves in the very last seats, at the very top corner of the television studio. We did not mind; we were out of the heat and finally sitting. Somewhat into the show the host enthusiastically announced that he needed someone to sing a song. My daughter, six years old, grabbed my arm and up went my hand. The game show's host looked skyward toward the balcony and his next words were,

"You! With the Frank Zappa mustache, come on down!" After singing an acappella version of the David Pomeranz song,

It's in Every one of Us, the host said, "Well, we have a profes-sional here, Mary, what do we have for our singer?"

"Well, Bob, we have either a cash prize hidden behind the cassette tape of the Little Mermaid, or Larry can choose what's in box number 1."

I chose the box and as you might have guessed, it contained a Sony Walkman.

Now throughout my life, when the Universe gives me a teaching or a little synchronistic miracle takes place, my spinal energy would open. It feels like heat and chills, joy, and exhilaration.

I have always taken it as the Spirits exclamation point on a lesson or significant teaching. For me, the lesson here was not just the Universe's support for my continued growth and work, but more interestingly an example of how literal the Universe can be. I have always been told by my teachers to be crystal clear and visualize exactly what I want. In this case, I got the Walkman I asked for. I soon found out that you cannot record into a Walkman' you can only listen to it.

Hilda would explain that the more focused your mind, the more quickly you can manifest what you ask for.

"For every thought is a prayer, kid."

As my new adage goes, be careful what you ask for and where you send your energy, particularly if you are an evolved soul.

COMMANDMENT 4

Thou Shalt Celebrate the Sacredness and Divinity of All Life: Cause no suffering - Buddha

"Today, more than ever before, life must be characterized by a sense of Universal responsibility, not only nation-to-nation and human to human, but also human to other forms of life."
Dalai Lama

Physics has brilliantly illustrated that all things are made of light, radiating at different frequencies, quick and slow.

A rock, your hair, a sweater, a plant, are all made from the same building blocks of light; they are all made from the same primordial material.

Deepak Chopra is fond of sharing the notion that since energy cannot be created or destroyed, it's simply recycled endlessly.

So, the air you're breathing and the food you're eating could be the recycled atoms of Buddha, Jesus, and Lao Tzu.

Good company.

Furthermore, light travels in waves and at certain times it has a particle nature.

It is this particle nature that so closely resembles the Asian concept of energy, Ki, Chi, or the biblical conception of Spirit, etc. The biblical passage, "You are made in the image and likeness of God," can be conceived here as literal science.

Jesus gives a testimony affirming the energetic makeup of this world when he says, "Look up in the tree and there I am; look under the rock and there I'll be."

It is all light in different forms.

When we say, "Walk into the Light", what we mean is "Adapt to a higher frequency".

Our evolutionary quest towards "the Light," or higher evolution/consciousness is one part of the Prime Directive.

It is part of our genetic structure and programming.

One day we will discover a gene that is responsible for fostering our drive to continually evolve (grow) and enlighten ourselves. Remember the Great Chain of Being, at one time taught by the Catholic church: from animal to human, human to angelic, angelic back to the One Absolute.

Human-to-angelic is a metaphor for our life's purpose, our next energy signature, the next mansion in my Father's house, where we are evolving to.

Our next destination after this human existence. What all this growth and destiny is about.

You don't have to take my word for it, it's happening right in front of your eyes.

Upright man, known as "homo erectus", appeared about two million years ago in Africa and Eurasia.

Millions of years is a long time to be inhabiting the planet.

Who knows how many billions of people and how many entire civilizations have come before us?

The most recent ice age occurred about 11,700 years ago.

Scientists now speculate that planet Earth was hit by a comet three miles wide.

Glaciers covered many parts of the Earth and most of the ice-age animals (saber-tooth tigers, mastodons, woolly-mammoths) became extinct in a mega die-off.

Pockets of civilization still existed and had to adapt to the harsh new reality.

To survive, the humans domesticated plants and developed grain storage 11,000 years ago.

The hunter-gatherer society eventually gave way to the more recent agrarian civilizations.

Apparently what saved human life was a rapid mental development.

The macrobiotic community say that cooked cereal grain was partly responsible for this mental development.

Grain was the very last evolutionary plant that developed.

The seed and the fruit were one and the same.

Grain grew straight up. The first in the edible plant kingdom to do so.

Kushi said, when early man consumed grain, he began to stand straight up as well.

When he began to cook the grain, the early human brain grew by leaps and bounds.

Grain breaks down slowly into a pure source of steady nutrition in the form most important for human life (glucose). In essence, the most evolved in the animal kingdom (most mammals, including us), derived the perfect source of nutrition from the most evolved in the vegetable plant kingdom.

I share this macrobiotic insight to accentuate the notion that the plant kingdom specifically evolved to support and feed the animal kingdom.

If you look at each stage of animal development, you will find the majority of animals deriving their nutrition from plants.

Apparently we are no different.

It is said that humans are the most evolved species on our planet.

There are times when I would question the veracity of that statement.

But the historical timeline of evolution is definitive.

We humans are the most recent mammal to come about.

As the most evolved animal, it is in our power to control the elements and all life on our planet.

All along the evolutionary path of consciousness, human contact, being the most highly developed in the animal kingdom, stimulates the development of all things.

Since everything is continually evolving on this planet from lesser forms of consciousness to greater ones, it is important to have compassion and understanding for everyone and everything.

Be patient.

Just like teaching a younger version of you in elementary school.

It takes time to train or mentor those species and mammals that are working their way up to humanhood.

If you believe that everything is evolving to a higher form, in theory, you are now the adult in the room.

This wasn't always the case and we have had a lot of help, too.

You have made the trek, lifetime after lifetime, scratching and chewing your way from lower forms to the magnificent present!

If you are reading this, I rest my case, Lassie.

Sometimes we have to help others along the way; lend a hand.

It's part of the prime directive to grow and help.

Consider yourself a mentor or a teacher.

Remember, this is a big school down here.

By promoting continual growth and teaching to those that are younger in consciousness, you are doing what we desperately need(ed) ourselves.

We'll call you Sensei or Sifu.

Doesn't make a different what you call yourself.

Reach down and lend a hand, acknowledge, become aware of, etc.

You are like a God to a plant, or insect, or animal, even a child.

Especially the handicapped.

So be beneficent, God-like.

Filled with compassion, patience and understanding for all life.

With a grandfatherly concern, bring your power and stability into the present.

And here is an original concept. When you pay attention, you bless all.

A simple glance or acknowledgment.

It's an energy and consciousness exchange, simple physics.

The Native Americans recognized and deeply respected the sacredness of all the things.

They felt all things were designed by the One Creator, who is made of the same sacred stuff.

In 1855, Chief Sealth of the Duwanish Tribe in the State of Washington, wrote the following in a letter to President Franklin Pierce.

He put it like this;

"All things are connected.

Whatever befalls the earth befalls the sons of the earth.

Continue to contaminate your bed, and you will one night suffocate in your own waste.

When the last red-man has vanished from the earth, and their memory is only the shadow of a cloud moving across the prairie, these shores and forest will still hold the spirits of my people; for they love this earth as the newborn loves its mother's heartbeat".

The concept that we can influence or mentor the things that come before also presupposes that we, too, are being mentored. This is the concept from the Great Chain of Being—from human to angelic.

Yes, I believe in a higher evolved order, too.

Ever feel the breeze from Archangel Michael's wings?

My teachers have all believed and taught about a hierarchy of higher evolved souls, egging us on, rooting for our continued growth and development.

You probably have a whole contingent of more highly evolved beings committed to you.

A byproduct of our own development is that we simultaneously spiritualize the earth's inhabitants towards its/their own natural evolution.

Thus, our journey down here is not just the enlistment of self, but the breaking down of illusion wherever one goes.

I tell folks all the time that my pets are apprentices to be human in a future incarnation.

Every living thing, including plants, continually vie for human interaction.

I believe human interaction speeds up their growth and provides the optimum environment for all things to grow. We have the power to free all things from their own bondage/nature.

I do not actually think you were an animal in a past life, unless it was an exceptionally long time ago.

But ever notice humans at a buffet?

Like pigs at a trough. Shoveling it in.

Perhaps a less evolved lifeform in a past life?

I don't know, but have you ever noticed how smart a ten-year-old dog is?

Perhaps as smart as a 14-month-old child?

Capable of simple reason and interaction.

And that brings us to Commandment,
"Thou shalt celebrate the sacredness and Divinity of all life."

Want to know a secret?

Everything needs to, wants to, is programmed to evolve.

All animals, regardless of how young they are, want desperately to live, and fear death, just like you.

Mammals can feel pain.

So, in conclusion, become conscious and provide the optimum environment for all things to grow.

I am free and I give freedom!

A side thought for your consideration...
To every growing thing, every living creature, interaction with humans is an apprenticeship towards humanhood.
That's why pets eventually interact consciously with their owners.
Even a simple weed that has given birth to a tiny yellow spring flower is vying for your attention.
Something as simple as your glance and transmission of your personal energy can have a profound effect on all living things, something as simple as that weed.
Perhaps as much as confirming its existence.
Remember, you are God to all lower forms of existence.
Why do you think plants grow so much better when they are talked to?

That simple exchange of chi can help that weed to fulfill its destiny to evolve.

You are a highly evolved soul and hold the key to life and death of all lesser frequencies.

Every interaction can be as sacred as a blessing.

COMMANDMENT 5

Thou Shalt Forgive

"At a certain stage, forgiveness takes over."
Tina Turner

I have been teaching meditation classes on a weekly basis since 1974.

Usually on the day of class, I would get inspiration for a lesson to share with my students.

On this given day I had no lesson.

I surmised that it would come to me, perhaps on my way to class.

With my coat on and guitar case in hand, I was leaving home when the phone rang.

It was my next-door neighbor Lori on the other end:

"Larry, I know you have meditation class tonight; I thought you must hear this story. It's about my friend, Denise."

Realizing that sometimes God talks to us through other people, I got my pad and pen and invited Lori to carry on.

"Some years back," Lori started, *"Denise had a falling out with her father. They were always very close, but they were so alike, invariably they would fight. Dad had a lot of expectations for his daughter. The arguments eventually got so bad that Denise decided to extricate herself from his life entirely, at least, she thought, for a time. They did not talk to each other, correspond, or even show up together at the same place for family gatherings. Their stubbornness with each other seemed to be insurmountable. Then, suddenly, her father had a fatal heart attack.*

Denise was completely unprepared for her father's sudden demise.

She thought there would be time to mend their riff but alas, the hand of fate changed everything."

The old biblical saying, *"I come like a thief in the night, you know not when"*, was never more real.

Now, Lori's friend Denise was in a very difficult place.

She opted for not going to the funeral.

In fact, she couldn't even find her way to console her mother.

She was paralyzed with her grief, angry with God, even more disappointed with herself.

Months went by. She was barely able to function, and then she got up enough courage to pay her Dad a visit.

She went down to the cemetery and found her Dad's plot.

After what seemed like hours of tears, ranting, and tearing at herself, she began to feel peace.

She told her father how sorry she was and how much she loved him.

She reminisced with him and before she left, she took out their lucky arrowhead from her pocket.

They found it together on a hike many years earlier, when she was young.

She had carried it throughout her childhood and now placed it on her father's grave.

Days later, she visited her grandmother at the nursing home.

Grandma, stricken with Alzheimer's disease, was barely cognizant on these days, so Denise would read to her and talk with her.

Unfortunately, it was a one-way conversation.

Grandma was no longer present. She was distant, almost comatose.

Denise was content just sitting by her grandmothers' side, when one afternoon something shocking happened.

Grandma sat up straight, looked Denise straight in the eyes and said, *"Your father wants you to know he loves you very much, too, and thanks you for leaving our favorite arrowhead".*

Then, as quickly as she had delivered her message, she lied down to be completely unconscious again.

There is no separation between the two worlds. Forgiveness can heal your heart's travail.

When you have gotten to the place where you have worked out all your unfinished business relationship-wise, then "today is a good day to die".

The great philosopher Krishnamurti said, *"Without freedom from the past there is no freedom."*

One day we were traveling with Hilda on a New York City bus.

For days prior, she was going in and out of mystical states.

This is not uncommon for spiritual adepts when they meditate for many, many years and for many hours every day.

On this given day, the bus was fairly crowded.

Directly sitting across from us was a rabbinical gentleman dressed in Hasidic garb, reading from a religious text.

Very uncharacteristically, Hilda began pointing at this man, exclaiming loudly, over, and over, "He is Pope Boniface, he is Pope Boniface"

As to not create any more of an embarrassment, we apologetically hurried Hilda off the bus at the next stop.

Sometime later that day, Hilda was much more grounded and began to tell us her experience.

She said this gentleman across from us on the bus was Pope during a time of religious persecution.

It was during his tenure as Pope that Jews were routinely attacked, maimed, and murdered.

While he did not instigate these events, he also did nothing to prevent or dissuade them.

He missed his opportunity to uplift and better his world from ignorance and darkness.

Hilda said his sacred contract was to spend three lifetimes deeply involved with Orthodox Judaism.

In this way, his assignment would widen his vision and bring him closer to his intended spiritual development.

To move along spiritually, you have to work out all your failed or unfinished lessons.

Thus, everything we are and will become can be influenced by our soul's history.

Perhaps it would be wise to begin the forgiveness process as soon as we are capable.

Holding onto serious unfinished lessons can lead to illness and misfortune.

If you can, make your wrongs right.

Clean your slate and realize that many of the experiences that plague your present existence can have their origins in some long distant past.

Hilda concluded her message by explaining that sometimes the only way to get past your labels down here is to come back each lifetime with a different religion.

Hilda loved Jean Katz, the Godmother of my son, Adam.
Jean also happens to be a revered medicine woman.
Grandmother Morningstar.

She wasn't always a holder of a sacred name.

Her secret has been to live each day teaching fully, intensely, and extracting every ounce of wisdom, its very essence.

She started her life born Catholic, was brought up Baptist, then converted to Judaism when she married.

She later immersed herself in Yoga and Hinduism, became a nurse, and was trained by the Church of Medicine. Next, she became a social worker and was freed by the Church of Psychotherapy. Later she was blessed by the Dalai Lama, studied Macrobiotic Taoism with total conviction, meditated at the Insight Meditation Center with the Buddhists, was specially chosen to be taught by a Cuban Santeria, and finally ran off with a Lakota medicine man.

Now Jean, is the director of a Native American Church, Turtle Acres.

She has lived so fully she is beyond all labels.

She is an Earth mother.

If you were to ask her what her path is now, she would tell you she is a member of the Church of Love.

Go beyond your petty little selves, your labels, and be free. "I am free, and I give freedom!"

Remember, every action has an equal and opposite reaction.

If you are experiencing tremendous travail, you might be able to shift your personal suffering by recognizing that you are paying off your karmic debts.

It could be from this life or a past one.

Of course, this presupposes that you believe in some form of reincarnation theory.

If you do, you are in the majority. Most of the world's population includes this karmic consideration.

If not, you might want to read Dr. Brian Weiss' book, Many Lives, Many Masters.

It is a very poignant and remarkable explanation of the whole process.

But consider this, it doesn't really make a difference who you were in your soul's past lives or even if there was one.

All that matters is this life. For those brought up in the Judeo-Christian faiths, that can be a helpful way to think.

However, the soul's continued evolutionary quest—reincarnation—best explains our unknown, unforeseen tragedies.

Like an infant succumbing to a terrible cancer.

An innocent child's death makes no sense to us.

It seems totally unfair and meaningless.

And yet, that might be all this little divine soul needed to do to graduate from this world of the little brainers and into the Light.

If you want to be free, you must come into the present and as difficult as it might be, let go of your past.

I'm sorry if that is insensitive.

Some folks have been violated so badly, they have a right to their pain and anguish for as long as they like, and no one should dispute it.

But eventually, they must let it go, if not in this lifetime, then the next.

We all must realize that even the most horrendous personal travail has a reason karmically.

And that karma might not be from this lifetime but from a past one.

That's what makes it so impossible to wrap your mind around it.

Sometimes it seems so unfair. And it is.

Be opened to learn from your mistakes and pay off your past debts (karma).

The sooner, the better.

Forgive yourself and forgive others that have trespassed against you.

Difficult as it may be, it is the way to freedom.

COMMANDMENT 6

Thou Shalt Love With All Thy Heart and All Thy Soul

"You don't fall in love; you rise in love." Hilda Charlton

"If you can come from your heart, you are going to win, win, win."
Paula Abdul

If love is the greatest power in our universe, then love is the answer to the question "how?".

When you finally know in your heart of hearts that you are truly the son or daughter of God, as the Essenes say, then love flows more naturally from you and it's your state of consciousness.

It's almost as if you are reacting in a God-like manner.

After all, if you are truly the daughter of God or the son of God, you have more than friends in high places; your parents are in charge of the whole shebang!

But you might never have that special relationship where you "actually know" that you are the eyes, the ears, and the voice of your Father/Mother in heaven.

Frankly, it does not make a difference. If you have honestly devoted your life to the work on yourself and have committed your life to doing good on the planet, then you are walking the walk.

You don't need a label.

Also, it doesn't make a difference if you just came to that conclusion yesterday.

What matters is NOW!

You do not need any religious affiliations to live a spiritual life and fulfill your destiny.

But priming the love pump and working on opening your heart, for many, makes the spiritual path much easier to access.

Hilda taught that the surest way to rise in meditation or, as she would say, "Go to God," was to rise or go up in love.

So Hilda would continually model behavior that would have heart opening consequences.

She would breathe, consciously focusing the breath in and out of her heart center.

She would breath in love then breathe out love to the world.

She said that when your heart opens, it's like a revelation and from that day on, whenever you take a deep breath, a smile will come to your face and you will be filled with ecstasy.

That's how you know your heart is open.

You have a direct heart-opening connection.

Hilda was continually teaching her students her spiritual heart opening tricks of the trade.

One evening, in her advanced Friday class, she started us out with a couple minutes of open heart breathing.

On that night, Ram Dass was in attendance.

Hilda said, ok kids, let's raise the vibratory rate in the room, shall we?

Visualize a nose in the center of your chest.

Now breathe love into your heart center, let a smile come to your lips and breathe love out to the world.

If it makes it easier for you, see the energy as a beautiful loving pink or a golden vibration filling every cell of your being from the top of your head to the tip of your toes.

Fill yourself with love.

Perhaps put a beloved deity on a golden throne you visualize in your heart.

That might be Jesus, Krishna, or any Master that you would like to align with vibrationally or feel close to.

If you do not feel a connection, then place a candle or simply visualize a light in your heart.

Now feel my words.

I implore you, my beloveds, fill our hearts with your love.

Oh my Lord, how much we love Thee.

Open our hearts this night and fill us with your perfection.

Now you advanced kids, go beyond my words, go deep inside and get your own lesson.

Feel it kids, feel the power and love from the Masters.

As the visualization continued, many of the advanced meditation adepts went way beyond Hilda's words and found themselves in a rarified spiritual state or rarefied "air", as Hilda would say.

Of course, all that breathing in love led us into a profound state of meditation and we continued for what seemed like hours.

The Light in that room was heaven.

As if God had come down.

At the end of the evening, Hilda reminded us that with passionate determination and practice, we would be able to hold that power and bring ourselves into that state of bliss without her intervention.

Then she reminded us that it is easier to access the Holy Spirit by being an heart-opened yogi than just about any other of the many paths back to the ONE.

How do you know your heart is open?

When your heart is open, it is not about you anymore.

It's no longer a personal issue or about your own personal success.

You feel directly connected to Spirit, with a love and kinship with all living things.

Often, you live in the moment, here and now.

You become acutely aware that you are living in an Interactive Universe.

A Universe that actually communicates with you, gives you lessons.

Wherever you go, you know you are sent.

You do not go to get something; you go to share.

All of life becomes an opportunity, a teaching.

Your life is about service, unconditional love.

You no longer see yourself as a victim, only as a vehicle for teaching, for healing, for uplifting and serving those you meet.

It was always your ego, your smaller self, that took things personally.

Your higher self can never play victim.

There will come a time when your heart breath and smile will fill you with bliss and everyone around you will be touched by this most wonderful of powers exuding from your open heart...LOVE.

You think outward.

As you come into your full unconditional power, you will begin to exude healing abilities.

Remember the secret of friendship is extending a hand, your love, your time, your wisdom.

The secret of love is to give love, the secret of healing is to do healing work.

Remember the Prime Directive on this planet, the reason you are here is to grow in every way possible and then to use that growth and wisdom to Serve, Uplift, and Inspire.

Simply stated, the purpose of life is to Grow and Help!

It is a Divine Madness...

So, this day, to begin the process of opening your heart, think outward and do your heart breathing exercise described below.

HOW TO OPEN YOUR HEART

For the next couple of minutes, on every in-breath, visualize a wonderful GOLDEN force of love entering into your chest and beginning to fill every cell of your body.

It starts with your imagination. Make believe.

I know you might be saying, "Well what does love look like?"

It is more like a force or vibration.

That is why I put a golden color to it. You can use pink if that works better for you.

Once again...

As if there was a nose in the center of your chest, breathe a golden force of love into your heart center, this moment.

Practice this right now.

OK NEXT...

On your exhalation, let a smile come to your lips and direct this force of love out to the world.

The smile at first is fake, but the sheer act of smiling dramatically changes the vibration.

So, breathe in Light, smile and send this love out to the world.

Keep repeating this exercise, breathe in love, smile...breathe out love and healing to the world.

If you like, lift your hands out in front of your body, as you breathe out. Direct the power to where it's needed.

Again, breathe in this pink or golden love into your heart center, put a big smile on your face...and breathe this love out to the children on this planet.

You'll know your heart is opening when you breathe this love into your heart and the smile comes on your face naturally, as in a blissful state.

With practice, you'll even feel your eyes blaze with an inner fire.

Now repeat it over and over again, and let your love shine until there is peace on Earth, or you are enlightened!

Love also has a scientific basis.

One that is part of our DNA.

The original Chinese science and philosophy explains our universe with this simple explanation,

"From the one Great Spirit come the two opposing forces".

The one absolute energy from the heaven's manifests on this planet into the two polar opposites.

From the One, come the two. Yin and yang.

This relationship of yin/yang, female/male, manifests itself throughout the entirety of our relative world.

So theoretically, love can be defined as the infinite attraction of opposites and a means for these opposites to achieve a greater balance by coming together.

And it's not just humans that experience this type of magnetism or love.

The age-old relationship of elements on the periodic chart of chemicals also exhibits the same characteristics.

Like the empty outer electron shells orbiting an atom.

Looking to bond with another element, trade electrons, and create a more stable relationship for both elements.

We might say that hydrogen and oxygen have been having a love affair, meeting each other's needs, since the dawning of time.

Their inherent attraction and exchange of electrons gives rise to water.

Being infinitely more stable, thus evolved, than either hydrogen or oxygen can be by themselves.

The same thing happens to us humans.

If you have unfinished business with the opposite sex, a parent or with a specific type of person, you might be highly attracted to someone that possesses the same characteristics as that person.

So, you can work out your junk.

How we interact and share our life energy with all things can foster or inspire growth and greater synchronicity.

In this quest toward higher union, humans see the opportunity manifest as a luminosity in the other.

A strong attraction.

When someone holds the key to greater balance for us, they just stand out like a street sign!

The highly charged chemistry between these two individuals is a signal that each possesses something the other needs to continue their growth.

We very often interpret this luminosity, this individual's special attraction to us, as sexual.

Which it probably is not. It is spiritual. It is about your continued growth and most of the time temporary.

Misinterpreting, often, an intimate relationship ensues.

After the sexual fireworks die down, the work that originally attracted you to each other can really begin.

Unfortunately, by that point the original lesson becomes much more complicated and very often completely misconstrued.

The intimate relationship could have taken you on a detour of sorts.

Perhaps we should read strong desire differently?

The original intense luminosity (attraction) you might have felt for each other could be nothing more than an indication that each of you holds a key to addressing your emotional blockages on your path to higher consciousness and eventual liberation.

Keep in mind, the stronger the ego's hold on each individual, the more painful the lessons are to overcome.

So, what seemed like relationship heaven initially, could appear more and more like relationship hell, in time.

Remember, attachment equals suffering; the greater the attachment, the greater the suffering.

Until you have gotten the lesson, having your buttons pressed is common and is an indicator that there is more work to be done.

What seemed like intense sexual chemistry, in reality, is about transforming your inequities and getting on with your personal spiritual development.

This significant other is a further means on your path and it might not be the fun and games you're thinking of.

Perhaps you can see it as another opportunity to get free and get healthy.

In a sense, we keep attracting into our lives the same lesson, the same types of people, until we get it and get over it.

Try this one....

SMILING BUDDHA Technique

Keep your legs shoulder distance apart, slightly bend your knees and keep your back straight. Stand with your arms outstretched in front of you as if you were hugging a tree trunk, arms in front, around shoulder height. Now breathe deep and rhythmically and empty your mind. I mean empty. Just work with your breath. In this exercise, your

strength comes from your emptiness. Attempt to feel no weight in your body, no weight from holding up your arms, no thoughts in your mind, just breathing, again...completely free and empty. Now with your eyes closed, smile, and see the Light in your forehead.

With your empty body and empty arms, continue hugging the tree, smiling, and seeing the Light in your head for at least five minutes to start every day. You will get strong physically, significantly boost your immune system, and the smiling remarkably has the tendency to open your heart. Try it.

COMMANDMENT 7

Thou Shalt Meditate

"Go into the closet and close the door."
"When thine eye be single, thy body shall be filled with light."

So how do we get to co-create?

How do we develop our personal power, so our life becomes profoundly meaningful?

Aligning yourself with the planetary power, your higher self is the key to this co-creation business. It takes an intensity of spirit and courage.

When you go inside, the way to harness your power is not by gathering or becoming more; it is by emptying what is already there.

By the emptying of your personal contents, you align with the source of all, the real power.

Ok, great words, now how do we do it?

To really learn how to meditate, you must start with calming your brain.

Our minds can be like a monkey jumping from branch to branch to branch. Sometimes like a thousand monkeys jumping all at once.

Do you routinely live in the future or past?

Join the club. You are not the only one.

While driving to the supermarket from work, you mentally plan out your shopping list.

In the market you decide what you are going to prepare for dinner.

While cooking, you ponder your evening's To-Do list.

While eating your dinner, you are thinking about a second helping.

During the second helping, you are thinking of dessert.

And so it goes, living in some future time scheme.

Controlling our thoughts, our mind, is difficult.

Living in the here and now takes a lot of practice.

There is an old cliche, *"The mind makes a terrible master but a wonderful slave"*.

When it is in control, it can be a whirlwind of thoughts.

When you train and focus it, it will respond with remarkable ability.

The Zen mind lives in the moment.

It's the old proverb that points to a truth, *"When washing dishes, just......wash......dishes."*

Living in the now takes practice.

When you develop this master organ and use it with focused intention, amazing things can happen.

As we develop and train our mind, our abilities continually blossom.

This is preparation for meditation.

Using the Breath to Achieve the Next Level of Mastery:

The breath and the mind are so closely interrelated that when you can control your breath, you can control your mind.

Consider you are breathing heavy. Panting. It is nearly impossible to concentrate with any efficiency.

The usual statement might be, "Wait a minute and let me catch my breath."

The average person can take in volumes more oxygen by paying attention to the breathing process and routinely breathing deep and rhythmically from the abdomen.

This, in turn, will enhance their entire being mentally, emotionally, and physically, preparing them for more refined spiritual endeavors.

Breathing exercises lower blood pressure and relax the musculature while simultaneously boosting and alkalizing your body It makes the mind sharper and more attentive. The body, in turn, burns hotter and the mind gets clearer. Breathing exercises are a mandatory prerequisite for deep, steady meditation and for spiritual living.

For starters, practice a simple yogic, alternate breathing exercise daily, regularly, and especially before meditation.

Hilda taught her entire class one of her teacher's special techniques. His name was Swami Mahadavananda. When Swamiji was in his 90s, he bade farewell to his students and admirers and went up to the meditation caves in the Himalayan mountains. A year later he returned looking dramatically much younger. Swamiji stated that his breathing exercise was a fountain of youth.

This is only part of the process he taught.

We do this exercise four times a day: upon waking, around lunch break, before dinner, and prior to sleep.

Three minutes each time. Make it a daily routine.

It's in the consistent, daily practice that you will see great improvement.

You will not believe the results!

Swami Mahadavananda Longevity Breath:
- As soon as you awaken, sit up in your bed.
- Put your right forefinger on your third eye. Cover your right nostril with your right thumb.
- Now breathe in for a count of 5. Close both nostrils put your tongue up to the roof of your mouth and bring your chin . . down to your chest. Hold and concentrate on your third eye.
- Slowly rise and breathe out your right nostril for a count of 10. Your exhale should be twice as long as your inhale.
- On the inhale your stomach should rise. Now breathe up . . that same right side. Close nostrils, chin down, tongue up, and concentrate on your third eye.
- Hold.... Slowly rise and breathe out your left nostril.
- Repeat this order again and again.
- Up left, hold, down right.
- Up right, hold, down left. In between, tongue up, chin down.
- All totaling three minutes.

Stop here....Try it now.

Once you have the hang of it, start engaging your mind with your breath.

You can put a color or a feeling to each exercise.

Breathe in love or breathe in light, healing, or peace, each one can represent a completely different vibratory rate (frequency), sound or color.

While you continue the Mahadavanda breath, visualizing in and out of the heart center is especially helpful.

Or you can surround yourself with a golden lining and breathe out your aura to about three inches completely around your body.

Breathe out tension and negative junk, or once you're really good at it, love to everyone you can think of.

You can cleanse yourself with your breath. You can heal yourself with your breath. You can make a difference in someone's existence by sending healing thoughts and intentions, again all with your breath.

- Repeat your three-minute breathing exercise sometime around lunch, even if it means going to the lavatory and sitting in one of the stalls.
- Repeat the exercise as soon as you get home from work, before you listen to your phone messages or attend to anything or anybody. Sit in a quiet space and close the door. You might want to put on some beautiful music. Three minutes again.
- And finally, perform the exercise once more before you go to sleep. Sit up, lean against the headboard, and do another three minutes. **Within a week, you will begin to see significant results.**

My father was a union plumber in New York City. Both he and his father, my grandfather, were in the trades. Grandpa built the Empire State Building; Dad built the World Trade Towers. He would take the IRT subway from the Bronx to lower Manhattan every day. His newspaper of choice for the morning commute was the *New York Daily News.*

It was an easy newspaper to read. One day, I asked Dad, "How come you never read the New York Times or the Wall Street Journal? All he said was, "It's too much mental work."

I understood. Construction work had difficult hours and tremendously fatiguing work. One week, however, on the breathing routine we just talked about and hopefully you tried out, Dad was reading the *NY Times* daily from cover to cover. After one month of the Mahadavananda breathing exercise, he was reading James Joyce.

After three months he began reading Yogananda's Autobiography of a Yogi! After six months, he was meditating regularly and no longer eating meat. He had a whole new lease on life.

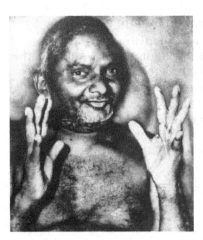

Swami Nityananda was Hilda's teacher.

Yeah, I know, intense. He was revered as a blessed saint in India.

His power was so focused, so extraordinary, that when people came to him for a special dispensation in the way of requests, they came away truly knowing that Swamiji was a bonafide representative of the divine.

He would sit outdoors under a great tree. Sometimes he would actually be up in the tree itself. Whatever the request, Nityananda would look into the heart of the supplicant, reach up into this sacred tree's foliage, and pull out a reply from God's storehouse.

Sometimes it was something tangible, like money or a talisman.

Sometimes it was an elixir to combat disease. Sometimes it was a special prayer. He was known far and wide as a miracle worker.

Nityananda wrote only one book in his life.

It was about the breath influencing the mind toward enlightenment.

When Hilda met Swami for the very first time, she was a young woman living in California.

These are her direct words, written by permission. Please see her amazing book, *Saints Alive*, published by Golden Quest.

"I first met Bhagavan Nityananda in Oakland, California. As a young girl striving to know the reality of life, I had no seemingly visible teacher to help. I was doing meditation and pranayama, breathing exercises, by myself, struggling day and night to still my mind and control my senses.

There is a saying, 'Take one step towards the teacher and the teacher will take ten steps toward you.' It is my contention that not one soul in this world, if it is pure in motive or sincere in effort, will go unseen or unheard, though there is often no visible outward sign. This proved true for me, and I believe I am no exception. For as I was striving to control the senses, the mind, the breath— wham—in the corner of the room there appeared a yogi with deep-set eyes half closed, sitting in contemplation in lotus position under a tree. Not a word was spoken, not a movement made by this yogi, yet grace came upon me instantly, and the breathing exercises and meditation became easy. It was a complete turnabout from the difficulties of sadhana into a peace.

This vision encouraged me to continue striving. It gave me an impetus to carry on by myself. The vision of the yogi disappeared from my room as quickly as it appeared. But the help I had so needed, the contact with a perfected soul, had come. I knew then my search was right and had not gone unseen by my then-unknown teacher. Someone had cared enough to reveal himself and help.

It was to be many years before I met him in the body and that again was his grace, for he drew me to him in a strange and wonderful way in India.

When in New Delhi, suddenly my mind came that point mentioned by Bhagavan Nityananda: it went wild. First, I thought, 'What is the use of all this sacrifice, this striving, this searching? Let me go back to the world.' And at that very moment my mind changed and all I could think about was getting to the land of Lord Krishna in Brindavan. I paced up and down the hotel room saying, 'I must see Krishna today or I will never see him in this life.' I rushed off to Brindavan, barely catching the train. Upon arrival, a man took me to his guru. Seated before his teacher, I was leaning back against the wall, and this teacher, who was a complete stranger to me, said sternly, 'Sit up.' I obeyed, and I felt a rush of power rise up the spine. When I met Nityananda later, he explained that he saw my mind had come to the fork in the road— to go on searching or to turn back to the Earth vibrations—and at that moment, through thought-force transference, he sent me to the other teacher, and the teacher knew I had been sent to him by Bhagavan Nityananda and gave the necessary help. The hierarchy of true perfected gurus has no separation, no jealousy, no 'me and mine' consciousness. They all work together for the betterment of humanity.

Later in a cab in Bombay, I saw a picture on the dashboard. It was dark, and I couldn't even see the details of the tiny picture, yet I felt impelled to ask, 'Who is that?' The cab driver answered, 'That is a great saint, thirty-three miles from Bombay in Ganeshpuri.' The next day I went to find the saint. I found him, and the search, inner and outer was over. And I even saw a picture of him sitting under a tree, exactly as he had appeared in the vision in my room in Oakland ten thousand miles away! Swami Nityananda told his close disciples, 'I gave her an experience in Delhi, and I introduced myself to her in a cab.' They asked, 'How could this be, Swamiji, when you haven't left here for twenty-five years?"

'Nityananda's very presence can change a person. There was no need for worshipping, talking, or lessons. The force emanating from his silence, one movement of his hand, and the nature within changed. My first sight of him as I lined up with a hundred people to walk one at a time before him was an experience I will never forget. I froze, the body went stiff, perspiration drenched me, and

all I could say inaudibly as I stood transfixed before him was, 'My beloved. My beloved.' My outward search was over. No need to look further. Peace and completion came within. The trail had ended.

He is a mighty man of God. I say 'is,' not 'was,' for even though he has dropped his body, his force of love never left the Earth and can be tapped by calling his name. I used to chant, 'Nityananda Satguru Maharaj, I am knocking on your heart."

So, it's time to start breathing, daily, regularly, and in particular just before you attempt to meditate. Breathing exercises like the Mahadavanda breath is the precursor to deeper meditative states and is the necessary preparation for a still mind.

When it comes to the world of the mind, I believe Jesus' most profound utterance was, **"...when you pray, go into thy closet and close the door..."** (Mathew 6:6); **when thine eye be single, thy body shall be filled with light."** (Mathew 6:22)

The Master here is giving the formula for connecting with your higher mind. His simple instruction: go inside and still your brain. When your mind is crystal clear, like a lake with no ripples, then you will be one with the Light within, your higher self. He was teaching us how to plug in to the Holy Spirit. Meditation is the hot wire to God. You can call it your higher self. Achieving this state of meditation is the doorway to the spirit world and one of the keys to self-mastery. Your daily meditation practice will eventually lead you to experience this profound oneness. When the Master further exclaimed, **"I and my father are one"**, he is talking specifically about this union. At this point, it is no longer about my little, ego self, but my much bigger, divine self. There is no separation, this state confirms the realization, the Light, is all encompassing, and I am... the Light!

Patanjali was the father of modern yoga. His observations codified yoga practice into the spiritual science of realization practiced by so many adepts today. His aphorisms on yoga have been translated many times. One of the most recognized translations is entitled, "How to Know God" by Christopher Isherwood. In this text, Isherwood shares Patanjali insights and wisdom on the meditative state.

"Concentration is a singular thought wave for a period of 12

seconds. Meditation is a singular thought wave for a period of two minutes and 24 seconds. No philosophies, no opinions, no thoughts, no mental movement, no physical awareness, just a continuous singular thought wave for two minutes and 24 seconds."

Think of the deepest sleep, the "dead" kind of sleep, where your brain just turns to **black**.

Now imagine being in that state of no mental movement, and being completely awake, focused, and conscious. Just clear, one-pointed, consciousness.

It can take years of dedicated meditation practice to reach this simple yet profound beginning. Just two minutes, 24 seconds.

But there is more according to Patanjali. After 28 minutes, 48 seconds of this continuous, unwavering meditation, you enter what Jesus referred to as "seventh heaven"—the opening of all seven of the body's energetic vortex's known in yoga as the chakras. You have seen pictures of saints; the halo around their heads indicates a completely open spiritual channel (the Kundalini). This state is sometimes referred to as **lower samadhi**. In this advanced state, the body goes rigor mortis—stiff and breathless with seemingly no heartbeat. The adept is in complete communion with God, or Spirit. You can read about these mystical states in many autobiographical texts written by these extraordinary souls.

Hilda was known as the teacher's teacher. From all over the globe, spiritual heavyweights, famous musicians, sensei's, swamis, monks, rabbis, ministers, priests, psychics, and more, came to Hilda with their personal spiritual questions. On one such occasion, a group of monks from the northwest United States trekked across the country for a private interview with Hilda. The monks belonged to a cloistered monastery. They conducted a very simple, rudimentary lifestyle consisting of farming, plant-based diet, prayer, and many hours of meditation. In fact, they regularly meditated long into the night. After about eight long years of this intensive, committed spiritual practice, the monks started experiencing pro-found states of samadhi but did not know what was happening. Reaching out to their church teachers and confessors was of little help. There was no one that could explain their breathless mystical state and their weird spinal fire. So, somehow, they were referred to the elderly meditation master in New York City.

That being Hilda. Hilda explained to the holy monks the details and significance of their experiences, referring them to historical members of their own church that had had similar profound experiences.

Now while this can sound "out there" to most of us, remember meditation is a lifetime practice.
The individuals that achieve these extraordinary spiritual states have been "sitting" for many hours a day, for years and years.

Every religious tradition has their representatives of this mystical advanced state or relationship with the "One". St. Theresa of Avila had many such experiences detailed in her confessions. The blessed Saint, after many hours of devout prayer and meditation, was discovered lifeless. Her body appeared stiff and breathless; thus, she was taken for deceased. Her flock proceeded in preparing her body for burial. One of the ritual customs was to fill in all the body orifices with wax. The purpose was esoteric—to prevent evil from gaining entrance into the venerated flesh of the deceased. While the sisters were preparing her body for burial, St. Theresa returned from this extraordinary spiritual state, and just in time. She explained that she was in communion with the Father. This happened on more than one occasion. Theresa asked the sisters to say nothing of the experience. She did not want to call attention to herself, and these were, after all, Inquisition times.

Imagine an inspired pianist, practicing and playing eight, even ten or more hours a day, for fifty years. We can easily understand how remarkable that musician might be. Listening to Maestro Vladimir Horowitz play piano like a keyboard angel masks the realization that he had dedicated his entire lifetime to get to that single moment. Intensive hard work, passion, and talent leads to magical musical prowess. When it comes to the mystical or spiritual achievements, there is no difference. Intensive practice evolves one to dramatically stand out. Padre Pio prayed and meditated 14 hours a day for decades before he received the stigmata. Rabbi Nachman was so filled with Spirit that his congregation would shield their eyes from his luminosity. There are few individuals who devote their entire life to spiritual pursuits. So, to us, these spiritually evolved souls may appear miraculous. To them, it is a lifetime of spiritual fervor and intense dedicated practice. In reality, it's achievable by many. Remember Jesus' wisdom, *"Far greater things you shall do, than I have done".* It's just so much easier in our society to become an expert plumber than it is to become an enlightened plumber.

There is one last, advanced state of Samadhi.
Patajali called it *Maha Samahdi or Nirvikalpa Samadhi.*
According to the Father of Yoga, Patajali, it takes five hours, forty-five minutes, and thirty-six seconds to reach this revered state.
Don't ask me how he knew. When this state is achieved, it can be a yogi's final conscious exit from this world.
It's the doorway to the next world. This communion is where *"Thy body shall be filled with light".* One becomes enlightened or simply *"in Light".* At this level, there is a choice: stay in this world or drop your body and meld into the Light. It can be a graduation ceremony from this world to the next evolution level.

Train yourself... study and work at it with fervor... "hell-bent for heaven," like Hilda used to say. Develop an unwavering focus.... Nourish your wonder. A powerful mind with intention, combined with an energetically open body, can create a vision-ary life, a life with conviction, a life worth living. Biblically and scientifically, all of existence is made of energy; energy that re-sponds to intention. Read this again and again!

Now Let's Review:

Training your mind with breath, prayer, and meditation pre-pares you to fulfill your dreams, take on your assignments, and fulfill your sacred contact. Striving to create an excellent mind is not only a gift you give to yourself but to the world. Use your mind to create an in-light-ened being, a visionary, yourself.

COMMANDMENT 8

Thou Shalt Have a Viewing Point

"In praise and blame, always the same"
Satya Sai Baba

"I was taken by the master for a journey on the inner plane. What you would call the dream world. The first stop was a dark, horrific place. What I would refer to as a hell world. The most horrendous things were around me, but I managed to pull in and didn't flinch for one emotional iota. By this point it was clear I was being tested. My goal was a master soul's ability of non-reaction."

Hilda

For Hilda's advanced Friday evening class in NYC, you were required to get Hilda's special permission to attend. This was her inner group, her inner sanctum. She wanted students that were intensely passionate about their spiritual development, students that had the zeal to choose God realization first and foremost. I was having such incredible spiritual experiences and insight from attending Hilda's other classes, I expressed interest in attending her Friday evening, Blue Card Class. Permission required a personal interview with Hilda.

Going to this additional class would mean driving into the city from the very end of Brooklyn (Coney Island) during rush hour. And this, after work as an Assistant Principal in a Flatbush, inner city school for children with special needs.

Hilda liked students with a spiritual fire. In fact, it was a necessary requirement to get close to her. We were so innocently inspired, so spiritually charged, that we did not even question the sanity of making such a trip. We ended up making that trip for years and years, and lovingly at that. Our youth fueled our fervor, and our fervor knew no bounds. We believed we were like Jesus' inner circle. We were thrilled to be involved with a real master soul, one who was able to read you like an open book. We were, to coin the title of Hilda's book, *Hellbent for Heaven*. This fire and spiritual longing are what futurist Barbara Marx Hubbard calls the "Hunger of Eve," the unquenchable hunger that fuels one's own personal quest towards God realization.

After some of us requested to attend her special class, Hilda invited us for tea at her small, ashram-like apartment. She graciously sat us down and served us with a special attention. She wanted to get a sense of who we were. While serving us an herbal concoction, she gently slipped in questions. They were directed lovingly and with wonderful humility. She had an infectious sense of humor that colored our visit with a cheery demeanor. As we answered her inquiries, we had the sense that she was cleansing us, consuming our psychic debris. We felt lighter and somehow renewed. It was quite extraordinary.

Hilda's interview followed along the lines of yogic chakra or energy field science. We discussed each world of chakras, their meaning, and how our personal world and relationships unfolded with them in mind. This was to be my first Hilda Charlton, full body "chakra scan". It was Hilda's version of a psychological, or better yet, spiritual evaluation. It was also to be another wakeup call about our plugged-up energy fields and how to address them. The chakras go something like this.

The first three chakras; survival (perineum), sexual (genitals) and power (around the naval, hara, Tan tien), maintain themselves in the psychological domain of the small self, EGO.

Ego here is defined as our separation from Great Spirit, our more evolved, unstuck, higher self.

Essentially these first three chakras are all about fulfilling ourselves, our needs, our opinions, our gratification, our security, our identity, our CORE stuff.

Me, me, me, me, my, my, my, ME.

The concept of "one" with the Universe does not apply here. It is the battlefield of the lower, desirous planes against the higher God self, so clearly written about in the Hindu text, *The Bhagavad Gita*. The Gita illustrates our personal separation from the one Spirit and the story of our journey back to the One.

Since the primary human motivations at this level of development center around these first three energy vortexes: survival, sexual gratification and power, the chakras give us the perfect explanation for the mess you might find yourself in down here.

This process of investing time and energy in separation is what scripture calls "maya" or illusion.

As long as we identify with the lower three chakras, we are personally separated from God.

The pain and suffering of that separation is "your lot in our life ".

Check out this quote from the textbook entitled, *From Heart of Hinduism.*

"Under maya's influence, the atman, (the soul) mistakenly identifies with the body.

He accepts such thoughts as "I am white and I am a man," or "This is my house, my country, and my religion."

Thus, the illusioned soul identifies with the temporary body and everything connected to it, such as race, gender, family, nation, bank balance, and sectarian religion.

Under this sense of false-ego (false-identity) the soul aspires to control and enjoy matter.

However, in so doing he continuously serves lower desires. In frustration he often redoubles his efforts and, compounding mistake upon mistake, only falls deeper into illusion."

When we arrive at thinking outward and using our consciousness and energy compassionately to uplift the world around us, we arrive at the fourth heart chakra, the energy vortex of **compassion, service, and love**.

Dr. Richard Alpert, a.k.a., Ram Dass, inspired so many on our spiritual journeys with his bestselling spiritual cookbook of 1971, *Be Here Now.*
Here's what he writes...
In regard to the spiritual leap of consciousness from the lower chakras to the **fourth heart chakra**, Ram Dass writes:

"If you had crossed the first great barrier (between the third and fourth charkas) so completely that all your energy was localized in the fourth chakra, then you would experience only the compassionate feelings of the brotherhood of the Spirit with all other beings.

Whether in a sexual embrace or in a business or social contact, the only feeling towards the other person would be of 'us-ness'. Since you would no longer have any investment in yourself as a lower separate ego entity, all of your actions would be in perfect harmony with all the forces acting in the field at that moment.

You would be living in the Tao."

When your spirit resonates with the **fifth chakra**, the throat center, truth in word becomes your power and ability. Your spirit has raised to a place beyond your "me" self and resides as a listening partner with higher awareness. It is then that your words will possess a special **"power"** capable of producing tangible results.

Whether using your word chi for healing, cutting through negation, or fulfilling the Prime Directive.

In time, with practice, you will develop an extraordinary ability. Conscious is a word that comes to mind here. The adept hears the words in his or her mind before speaking and possesses the unique ability to choose the correct words to reach the listener profoundly.

Synonyms such as alert, attentive, awake, and responsive, give us a clearer definition of an individual with an open fifth chakra.

The opposite state might be defined as being unconscious, as in unconscious babble spewing from our lips.

Many sadhus (spiritual adepts) take a vow of silence to cultivate this chakra.

Hilda's mantra for opening this chakra was **"KYBMC,"
meaning, "keep your big mouth closed."**

The sixth chakra, located in the forehead, is about wisdom, God's mind, wisdom. Infinite.

Your thoughts possess the same unique abilities your words do.

Your thoughts make things happen.

This higher mentality creates thoughts that can be tangible, that are things in and of themselves.

Not in league with your smaller desires, but a higher resolve.

This is Jesus uttering, "I and my father are one."

One mind.

"As a man thinketh, so shall he become."

The seventh chakra is about illumination.

When all seven energy vortexes are open, we become a fully functioning human.

The halos you see around pictures of holy ones signify this achievement.

Also, the medical caduceus, the insignia physicians sometimes wear on their garments, is a metaphor of this enlightened state. . You've seen this insignia many times, perhaps without knowing its true meaning. Two snakes curling up a main staff and at the top, spreading out like wings.

It is said that the spiritual channel, located in the spine, and called the Kundalini, functions and looks like the caduceus.

Before we go back to Hilda's kitchen and her interview with us, let's pause momentarily to do some chakra self-reflection.

After reading the explanations of each chakra below, I

want you to consider how much of your life is influenced and controlled by that chakra?

Be honest with yourself.

FIRST CHAKRA—"SURVIVAL"

Energy vortex found around the base of the spine.

Think of Darwin's *Survival of the Fittest* theories, his explanation of man's eternal quest and the instinct for survival/security. This first charka represents a basic ego driven desire.

Think of Abraham Maslow's *Hierarchy of Needs* and recall the psychologist's explanation that all humans need to have basic needs fulfilled to continue growing.

It's easy to be a victim of this chakra, especially if you've been humiliated, violated in some profound way, or have gone without.

Especially if it happens early in life. Not to mention living under tyranny. And it is easy to be filled with fear. Just consider the unemployment line or a hungry child. It is easy for life's cruelties to stunt one's psychological growth. Sometimes the wounds are so deep that if we heard the story, we might agree that they have an excuse for their life being a big mess. A good excuse. Unfortunately, there are many who have a great deal of their life and personality invested in this chakra, which is a main motivating factor in being separated from higher consciousness.

This chakra usually feeds separation, being all about me. It's tough to be stuck there. If you have ever worried about making ends meet or have not eaten for a couple days, you have spent time in this chakra's energy field. Is it possible that you are a victim of this chakra? What percentage of your life energy are you still spending here?

SECOND CHAKRA—"SEXUAL"

Think of Sigmund Freud as the spokesperson for this energy center. He believed that human motivation can be reduced to sexuality. And sexuality is the prime mover at the base of all human interaction.

How do you use your sexual energies?

Are you aware that sexual energy can also be creative energy?

Do you, or *have you*, used your energy, charm, or sex appeal to manipulate someone?

How about in business?

Do you think in terms of sexuality?

Do you live in a secret world or keep secrets that no one knows about?

Are you aware of the inverse relationship between sexuality and spirituality?

How much of your energy is used to maintain this chakra?

Are you a victim of this chakra?

What percentage of your life energy are you spending here?

THIRD CHAKRA—"POWER"

Think of Freud's contemporary, Dr. Alfred Adler. Adler disagreed with Freud's analysis that sexuality was the main motivating factor in life. He believed the main motivating factor is power and the desire for *superiority.*

How do you use your power?

How do you interact with the world?

Do you try to take advantage of people?

Do you like to control people?

Does your ego often need to be right?

How about being right by making others wrong?

Do you use your influence to achieve your own agenda, maybe for your own aggrandizement? (Look it up.)

Are you a victim of this chakra?

What percentage of your life energy are you spending here?

FOURTH CHAKRA—"THE HEART CHAKRA COMPASSION, SERVICE, LOVE, GRATITUDE"

You know your heart is open when...

You become acutely aware that you are living in an Interactive Universe. You feel directly connected to Spirit. Every deep breath is a chest full of love followed by a smile. You live completely in the moment. What Hilda Charlton called a "die mind." Wherever you go, you know you are sent. You do not go to get something; you go to share something. All of life becomes a teaching opportunity. Your life is about service and unconditional love. You no longer see yourself as a victim. It is your ego, your smaller self, that takes things personally and reacts negatively. You are about your Father/Mother's work.

It's no longer a personal issue.
It's no longer about your own personal success.
It is a Divine Madness...

How much of my day is dedicated to helping, serving, loving, supporting, thanking?

Now let us get back to Hilda's kitchen.

As we traveled up the spine's energetic pathway, exploring our psychological connections and nuances from chakra to chakra, we started rising. The vibration around Hilda was filled with luminosity and she encircled us in her web of Spirit. Time slowed down. It almost seemed to stand still.... creating what can best be described as a "spiritual instant". James Joyce described the experience as "quiddities"—the perfect moment of realization, of awareness, of aliveness. What the Japanese refer to as Satori—a flash of sudden awareness. We were in Truth, receiving Hilda's preparation, an initiation into her mystery school.

By the time Hilda got to the sixth chakra with us, my usually scattered monkey mind was profoundly quiet and one-pointed.
But the beautiful solitude internally earmarked the realization of my dire need to meditate more deeply and more regularly. By the seventh chakra, Hilda smiled and told us it was indeed attainable.
At the end of our interview, Hilda handed us a blue rectangular card. In the middle of it was an equilateral triangle with a dot at its center. Hilda hugged us with wide arms exclaiming, *"Welcome to Friday Night Class, kids!"*
I will always remember the love in that hug.
Love was Hilda's greatest power.

It was a chilly, deep Fall Friday evening in NYC. Hilda wanted us to build up "the vibratory rate", in the room. One hundred people sitting on a sky-blue carpeted floor, breathing, chanting, singing, and getting the cobwebs of the day out of their system. Hilda usually began by scanning the room. After so many years of inner spiritual work, her skills at reading were x-ray like. It was another of her siddhi (powers). Like cleaning our hands before dinner, we routinely would clean off our auras before coming into Hilda's presence. It sounds a bit strange, but she had the ability, or gift, to plainly read you. Uncanny. After all issues were settled, she would begin talking, sharing an inspirational anecdote, cajoling us to excel in our spiritual practice. A short time later, she would kick into her mastery training, like a marine boot camp for spiritual teachers. She wanted her students to embrace and channel through their higher self-24 hours a day! She was a spiritual surgeon, and your ego was the cancer. Receiving an ego-ectomy from Hilda was considered a great blessing from the master. In this class, you were expected to walk like a master soul, talk like a master soul, open your heart at will and have the supreme courage of a warrior. She would literally teach you how to keep your head in the clouds but your feet on the ground. As Swami Yogananda used to say:

"Believe in a miracle, kids...
Renew yourself by the renewing of your mind...
Go beyond your little selves...
let go, kids...let go and let God!"

Her lessons had an extraordinarily deep effect in this environment.

The energy in this room was powerful, hypnotic, and tangible.

Hilda was a master at invoking the Spirit.

Like a Native American shaman banging at Spirit's door, pleading with chants and drumming for Wankantanka (Great Spirit) to open the floodgates of blessing.

We felt what we called the Holy Spirit tugging at our hearts, undoing our hardened conditioning like the peeling of an onion skin one layer at a time.

During her meditation,

Hilda gave an impassioned plea to her students to go beyond their little petty reactionary egos.

She said we had to stop allowing the outside world to decide for us how we felt.

We could no longer afford to choose *"The luxury of whoa."*

By choosing to be a victim, the terms of our happiness were being dictated to us.

It would compromise our health, both physically and spiritually.

I remember her saying something like this:

"Tonight, those of you ready to undertake the next step in your personal spiritual journey must make a vow, a vow not to give away your power through a negative reaction. By continually

reacting, you give away your power. Same as being manipulated
like hamsters on a treadmill.
   I want you to learn how to hold your center even in the midst of
chaos.

   Those of you who are ready to take this next step.
   Only do this if you are sure you are ready to be tested.
   If yes, then repeat the following with me three times.

   I will stop reacting!
   I will stop reacting!
   will stop reacting!
   Now it's time to live it, kids!"

   Just before we left, Hilda reminded us that by taking that
vow, we were going to be tested.
   GET READY.

   It is said, when you take one step towards the masters, they
take ten steps toward you.
   I did not have to wait long for the masters' arrival and my first
test. That night, on my way home from class, it happened. I was
driving an eleven-year-old car, a big seven seat Mercury Monterey
with a 390 cubic inch engine and only a two-barrel carburetor.
   Slow and sluggish to pick up, but once it got up a head of
steam, it cruised. We had just moved to New Jersey, and I was still
unfamiliar with the roads. Forty-five minutes along Route 80 West,
flashing lights and noise started screaming up from the engine.
I pulled off the side of the road and cautiously opened the hood.
In the pitch black of a damp and overcast evening, all I could see
were sparks flying in cadence., All I could *hear* was a loud banging
noise. To make my test all the more interesting, the flashlight I
was carrying in the glove compartment had dead batteries.
   Here I was, 1:30 am, in the middle of who knows where?
   I remembered Hilda's warning and smiled.

   After all, I did ask for this and in fact vowed in my heart of
hearts not to react.
   I came from a neighborhood and family that was chief
amongst reactors.
   My father was a nuclear reactor. When he worked and encoun-
tered adversity, every other word from his lips was *"son of a*
bitch." It is safe to say that in this working-class neighborhood,

life's hardships brought out humanities' baser nature. It was an eye for and eye, a dent for a dent, simple, clean cut and emotionally impaired. And my emotional maturity was similar to that of my father's. If I was challenged, I would play the victim. Like a child throwing an emotional hissy-fit. That way I did not have to pay attention and I always had an excuse for my childishness. It was usually *their fault, her fault, God's fault*, but certainly *not my fault*.

Now back to Route 80. There was no improvement or resolution in the big Merc; it continued its noise, banging, and sparks. I really did not know what to make of it and I was about 15 minutes from home. So I decided to vigorously chant and pray my way home. Fifteen minutes and a lot of Hari Om's later, I pulled around the back of the garden apartment complex to my designated spot. The parking area was poorly lit and situated on a deep incline. It pitched backward, off a small cliff, down the side of a steep hill. I parked and shut off the engine. Well..., at least I *tried* to shut off the engine. The car started convulsing and spitting from its two exhaust pipes. With a gnashing, farting, whirlwind of sound, I had to think quickly. It was early morning. I did not want to wake the entire neighborhood. I immediately turned the engine back on and sat there to regain my composure and think of what to do. I was reminded of one of Dad's instructions about handling serious exhaust emission problems. He used to say, "Simply shut the engine off while the car is in Drive". So, I pressed the emergency brake to the floor and shut the car off while it was still in Drive. It worked like a charm. No backfires, just the instant silence of the sleepy lake garden apartment community. Relieved, I got out of the car, took my things and went into my apartment.

I, however, forgot to put the car into *Park*!

Five-thirty Saturday morning, Butch my neighbor from the apartment upstairs called me.

"Larry, I'm sorry to call you so early. Have you seen your car? Maybe you should look out your window."

Sure enough, the old Merc was dangling off the side of the cliff, doing a 4,328-pound, high wire balancing act. Normally when confronted with screaming reality, I would throw a whining, cursing, temper tantrum.

Just like dad. Yet this was the spiritual test Hilda had promised, my moment of moments. I had the power of choice, and up from my larynx rose a verse that I sung to the We Five's famous song, *Woke up This Morning.*

"Woke up this morning, my car was off the cliff....iff...if, myyy car... was off, the cliff...if... I got troubles, whoa, whoa, I got worries, whoa, whoa, I got wounds to bind."

At that moment I grew up.

Getting upset was not going to change the circumstances; it would only make me jump through a hoop of emotion like a trained dog. I would still have the deal with the car and perhaps an ulcer or the start of something even uglier. I called the tow truck. He arrived in twenty minutes. I told him my story of sparks and fury from the night before. He pulled the car back up and opened the hood. Apparently, the mechanic from the very recent tune-up forgot to tighten the spark plugs. When the engine was running, the plugs blew out of the crankcase and miraculously stayed attached to the cable wires.

But the real miracle was that I was back in bed within the hour and there was **No Reaction!**

When I awoke, I was aware that I had passed the first leg of my vow—*I shall stop reacting.*

I was elated.

I had *decided* how I was going to feel and how I was going to use my energy.

Throughout my life, I was on the treadmill of happy/sad, happy/sad, like an emotional puppet.

This time I did not give away my power, and I had the volition to hold my center.

My former excuse, that God was using me as his personal doormat, was just what it sounds like—*ego whining.* Because I chose not to challenge my immune system and explode holes in my energy field, I turned into an actor instead of a *reactor.* Hilda said Pericles, the great Greek orator, was a Master soul because *he determined* his responses spontaneously to the circumstances in which he lived. For a second, I imagined what it must be like to possess Pericles' continued steadfast strength and conviction.

In the early 1980s, I was the treasurer of Physicians for Social Responsibility, Morris County Chapter. This was an organization with thousands of physicians united across America to call attention to and eliminate the threat of nuclear proliferation and eventual annihilation. I was on my way to The Medical Society of New Jersey in Trenton to give a presentation and lead a discussion on the movie *"War Without Winners"*. The movie was a devastatingly powerful treatise about nuclear holocaust and the game of "chicken" taking place amongst nuclear powers. At that time, the game was primarily between the U.S. and the former Soviet Union. This was to be my second major test on the "I will not react" vow, and it came on my way to that very presentation.

For some reason, at that time in my life, my Guides chose my most important spiritual tests to be around my automobiles. It was the year of the Chrysler bailout. Plymouth combined technology with Japan's Mitsubishi Corporation and came out with a sports car called the Plymouth Sapporo. It was a slick and fast automobile. On my way to the presentation, I was following my dear friend and my child's godfather, internist Dr. Henry. We shot down the parkway, two new cars blaring, when suddenly my car sputtered and died. Dr. Henry, aware of my travail, pulled to the shoulder and backed up half a mile to where my car rested. We agreed that he would show the movie and call AAA for me. This was before cell phones. When the tow truck came, the mechanic popped the hood and took a long look. He turned to me and said,

"New car?" *"Yes"*, I muttered, obviously frustrated.

He said, *"Let me ask you a question. Do you have a good sense of humor?"*

That question seemed to cut my tension.

I giggled and nodded as if to say, *"What do you know that I don't?"*

He said, *"Your engine has seized"*.

"Whaaa?" I gargled.

"Your engine is seized! Where do you want me to tow it?"

After *a quick adjustment of mind*, I directed him, *"Let's bring it back to my dealer"*.

Therein began the saga of the Mitsubishi engine.

Apparently, my car came with a birth defect.

When the engine got hot and expanded, the oil crankcase bolt melted down.

The oil emptied from the pan onto the highway, leaving the engine without sufficient lubrication, thus the eventual engine seizing meltdown.

It took a whole season for the engine to be replaced by the dealership.

The whole *winter* season!

The loner cars the dealership gave me to drive were the famous Plymouth "K" cars without snow tires.

"K" cars with an attitude.

The first car's windshield blew in while I was driving.

The second had a tire that flew off.

Did I say *tire*? I meant to say, the *whole wheel* with the tire on it.

I spent the entire winter season with "K" car reliability. I am being facetious when I say that. Loners...

Early on, I recognized that I was being tested.

It was so obvious that it was comical.

This was a green beret boot camp for spiritual wannabees.

I should have written that song, *Hit Me with Your Best Shot*.

The service from the dealership was an abomination.

But with Spring came the flowers and my engine.

The very last day of the test, I calmly thanked the smirking head of Service, both of us knowing full well it was to be my last visit.

On my way out, a kindly, older gentleman from the Parts department pulled me aside.

"I know we'll never see you again." He said, *"And I certainly can't blame you, after the way you were treated.*

May I say you were an inspiration to me."

I looked at him deeply as he continued, *"I have never seen a person stay so cool, remain so kind, and after the kind of shit-storm you went through last winter. What's your secret?"*

Up from my larynx came,

"I recently decided I wasn't going to allow the outside world to decide for me how I felt for the rest of the day.

So, I made a vow to stop reacting. You guys were my greatest test so far".

I thanked him for his kindness and for paying attention.

One of my favorite sayings is that God talks to us through other people.

His comment was like a mystical confirmation from God, *"Job well done, kid".*

My next vehicle was the original Dodge minivan.

Guess where I did not buy it from?

I may not have reacted, but I was not an idiot.

The difference between us and God is that *"We have a point of view, and God has a viewing point".*

The idea of manipulating the Universe for our own happiness is just one model of existence.

And it smacks of an adult temper tantrum.

If you hold tribal beliefs, as well as strongly held opinions and ideologies, you are likely to experience the pain, torment, and suffering of life.

Especially if you believe those beliefs need defending and protecting.

So in reality, you are bound to be disappointed when your expectations are not fulfilled.

For instance, if a rainy day can depress you, you have a victim mentality. You can be *had*, manipulated.

Perhaps it is a control issue. Not having your model of existence supported can be very threatening and for some, frightening.

We hold onto our secure-seeming reality to give our world a sense of solidity.

It is our nature to seek a secure world with manageable boundaries.

It is quite unnerving when you realize that there is no solid universe, no boundaries.

In fact, the only solid on this planet is change itself.

So, if you are flexible and can adapt to whatever circumstance you find yourself in, you will be golden.

As physicists point out, there is no matter, just particles of light moving at different frequencies.

Michio Kushi would say this world is ephemeral, incorporeal. If you look hard enough, you could see between the lines. If you want to be more like God, just observe life unfold without exercising your ego's security need to categorize and label every experience as good or bad. Manipulate your own mind and be happy and at peace with what is unfolding.

What Will Make It Easier for You to Do This?

Acknowledging in an interactive Universe, the fix is in for everything to unfold specifically by design for your own growth and development. That would mean you are special and there is a universal intelligence or a science that is afoot.

Here's another gem...
If you really want to know what is, first remove what you think is.

Every opinion you currently have is the sum of all the programming/conditioning that you have had since birth.

Having an original thought means you must get yourself out of the way first. That is a lot harder than you might think.

Initially our mind is a blank slate that gets filled like a computer with all of life's information: your parents, family, teachers, churches, experiences, organizations, training, movies, books, peers, etc. Original thoughts and inspirations, free from our life's involuntary personal programming, come through us, not from us.

You must move your opinions and conditioning out of the way to see what is left.

Krishnamurti, the great Indian seer of the 20th century said, *"To know what is, you must first deprogram what you think is, all your preconceived notions."*

When asked 'How do you deprogram what you think are your preconceived notions?'

Krishnamurti quipped, *"Meditation, it's not what you think."*

The Third Patriarch of Zen states, **"The path of enlightenment is easy for those who have no preferences."**

When you have no opinions as to how you would like things to turn out, you are free.

Our suffering equates with our attachment.

Attachment equals suffering.

Our need to determine the outcome, our holding on to how we expect things to turn out, our ego's need to control the outside events, all lead to our personal pain.

Furthermore, the greater the attachment, the greater the pain and suffering.

Seng-T'san said it like this:

"If you wish to see the truth,
then hold no opinions for or against anything.
To set up what you like against what you dislike is the disease of the mind."
Hsin Hsin Ming by Seng-T`san

How do you know you're attached, stuck?

Simply.... When your ego investments are threatened, you get your buttons pressed.

We understand the challenges aging represents to the physical body.

Rigidity to change and inability to adapt is spiritual aging. What Hilda used to call "Earth Disease."

She would say the world has knocked you around so much that you have lost your capacity to make a quick adjustment of mind. She would remind her students that the rock standing rigidly in the middle of a raging river would eventually be ground to sediment. The water which always flows freely, flexibly, would weave and dodge around the obstacles.

Then to make the point, Hilda would have her class sing:

Row, row, row your boat,
Gently down the stream,
Merrily, merrily, merrily, merrily,
Life is but a dream.

The ego in consciousness philosophy is usually characterized as the lower, animal instincts and desires. With continued spiritual work and aspiration, our consciousness expands, and our kundalini literally evolves up the spine. The small ego-driven self gives way to a higher, profoundly more mature expression. When this energy reaches the fourth chakra, the heart or love center, we begin to loosen the grip of our ego-driven self-centeredness, attachment, and insatiable desire. It is at the fourth chakra that we begin to think outward, becoming sensitive to the greater scheme of things and our role in the interactive Universe.

The freedom to continually re-invent how we present ourselves goes beyond our attachment of who we believe we are. In the formative stages of spiritual development, we have the need to relate very strongly to our labels. Our professions, marital and economic status, our religious and political affiliations, etc. They define our reality, lending us solidity, stability, security. **After all, what is in you that causes you to feel threatened?**
Who, in you, needs a secure, controlled environment?
Isn't it the neurotic, smaller ego self, separate from the God self?
There's a rumor out there that you and I are the **Sons and Daughters of God.**

Talk about friends in high places.

Dr. Timothy Leary, the Harvard professor, wrote a treatise on the psychedelic journey that can be used as a metaphor to understand the concept of shedding one's ego. Leary called the stages/levels of the LSD experience "bardo's".

His explanation was based on clinical observations of actual LSD experiences.

Leary was a genuine explorer of consciousness.

In the initial stage of a trip, called the first bardo, the individual begins to get high.

As in any type of high, things gradually become humorous, raucous, and essentially less and less under control. Eventually the trippee begins to shed his/her grounded mortality and identification with all thing's ego.

Things like labels: "My name is Larry. I am a father of three, a school director, a teacher, a musician, a massage therapist, a minister."

With LSD, as the drug takes hold, it speeds up the human vibration, increasing the mind's spiritual frequency. It's at this time that our identification with all things "us" loosens even more profoundly.

In the second bardo (stage), Leary discovered that many people have the proverbial *"Bum trip".*

The inability to let go of their seeming solidness (ego) and the struggle to maintain control creates a difficult battle.

In, *The Psychedelic Experience,* Leary, Metzner, and Alpert put it like this,

"For the unprepared, the heavy game players, those who anxiously cling to their egos, the struggle to regain reality begins early and usually lasts to the end of their session."

Some lose to their ego's fear of losing control and literally can *"wig out".* Those that can make the transition, by letting go and loosening the ego's grip, can relax into a magical world of mind exploration and later, the possibility, for seasoned explorers, *"that of complete transcendence."*

Quoting from the Psychedelic Experience again,
"Beyond words, beyond space-time, beyond self.
There are no visions, no sense of self and no thoughts.

There is only pure awareness and ecstatic freedom from all game (and biological) involvements."

Leary, Metzner, and Alpert

We are learning to let go every day, slowly, much, much healthier, without the need for a drug. As Ram Dass puts it, *"The goal is to be high, not get high."* Being high is the freedom to be and explore without the fetters of our ego's fear of losing control. It is the concept of *"Letting go and letting God".*
While a psychedelic experience may seem cool to some, it is like putting 1,000 watts of electricity through a hundred-watt bulb.
It fries your brain chemistry and very often leaves you depressed and empty.
Learning how to get free is a lifelong process.

Ram Dass' guru, Neem Karoli Baba Maharaj, in the 1960s said, Americans are so hardened materialistically, they need this violent stripping of their ego via artificial means as in psychedelics to see that Spirit governs all things.

Native American shamans similarly have used psychedelics to introduce their followers to the world of Spirit.
I believe, for most, it is unnecessary to move so fast.
Hari Dass Baba says, **"You can't strip the skin off a snake before it's ready to shed."**
Shedding is a natural process.
Remember St. Francis' words, *"Day by day, stone by stone, build your church slowly."*

So here is what you have to do to turn around the victim pendulum.
Think of this world as a planet that houses mental patients. Everyone here, including your significant others, have emotional handicaps and baggage of some variety.
If we were walking through a mental institution and individuals there were cursing at us in an extraordinarily rude way, I might say to you, *"Don't listen to what they're saying, they're crazy."*
That's the condition of this world and its inhabitants, "Casa loca crazy".

The Lesson to be learned here
When people can press your buttons, they are showing you places in yourself that need improvement.
Remember, nobody can make you feel bad without your consent.

1. So, make a list of all the people or circumstances that really get to you.
As you list them, you will find your patterns and old tapes repeating over and over.
And if it is **pressing your buttons**, you can be sure it's threatening your ego's security.
Your small, neurotic, separate-from-God self-ego security.

2. Now develop a strategy of how you are going to respond to each one of those circumstances (suggestions to come). Be patient; you must continually practice each strategy until you get it right. Turn it into a spiritual game. Let us see if Uncle Frank can press my buttons this year at the holiday party. You know when he greets you by saying something about you looking pregnant? **Work on your strategies.**

If you have ever taken an assertiveness training program, you know you have a right to say "no" without an explanation.
You have a right to remove yourself from an undesirable situation.
You have a right to be treated with respect.
If a person wants you to get a message, they have to say it in a way that you will be able to hear it.
If the truth is spoken, kindly and helpfully, it is obviously easier to get the message.
So, the question is, do they really want to communicate in an honest and sincere manner, or do they just want to emote, make you wrong and mix it up?
Consider if you are spoken to rudely, with an accusatory blanket statement, it is usually the latter—they just want emote, make you wrong, and fight.
Just respond by saying, without reaction, *"Thank you for sharing your insight, I will definitely give it some thought,"* and then go about your day remembering what we said about giving away your power in the crazy house.
When somebody is looking to tangle, looking for a fight, remember what the sound of one hand clapping is—silence. It takes two to tango.

Do not be suckered into fighting; it will just drain your power. When folks speak to you with daggers, that is their problem. They must live with that ugly vibration. It will permeate their being.

If you react to it, it will permeate yours. Who wants to live in self-created bondage?

There are many strategies that work to create a favorable relationship based on mutual respect. They do not always work, but they are worth a try.

Do not be lambasted by anyone.
If someone is treating you poorly, respond by telling them they are hurting you, maybe saying one of the following:

"If I said or did something that hurt you, it was not my intention.

I would like to discuss this with you, but you are clearly not in any temperament to do that now, so let us discuss this later when you are in a better place to just talk."
Then immediately leave the room.

Or

"I'm sorry you are so upset, and I'd really like to make this right for you and us, but I can't let you talk to me so rudely. Let us discuss this later when you're cooler and can speak to me calmly and with more respect."
Then immediately leave the room.

Always consider if their argument has any merit.
Be honest. *"Is this my problem or theirs?"*
If it is *your* problem, develop a strategy and change!
If it is *their* problem, thank them for sharing that with you and tell them you'll give it some thought.
Your response is the same for either.
"Thank you for sharing that with me. I'll give that some consideration."
Subject and discussion over. Now go about your day.

Remember some of the time-tested pearls of conduct.
"He that humbles himself shall be exalted,"
"Be all things to all people,"
"A mystic meets at a point of agreement,"

"Agree with thy adversary lest he rend thee," etc.

Every time you give into your lower emotions, addictions, and the negative vibration around you, you create a hole or leak in your vital energy. Like a continually dripping faucet, your chi leaks, lowering your immunity and making you susceptible to outside negative influences. It is like creating a hole in your aura, a chink in your armor. Remember, Dracula can only enter a household in which he is invited. With these thoughts in mind, you have a formula for continual growth. Every day we are getting input about where to put our attention regarding our Spirit. **Our higher self or inner voice mentors** our lower "stuck" self and shows us what we need to work on.
Listen; pay attention!

When the outcome is not to your liking, when your expectations are not fulfilled, it hurts.
Can you have an opinion without the hurt, without attachment?
We know opinions really seem to be needed when the stakes are high or lives are at stake.
Then we need to ask the age-old Native American question, ***"How do the actions we take here today affect the next seven generations?"***
If it affects them negatively, then you have your course of action based on what is correct, not based on your opinion.
You set out on a course of action because it is the correct course, not simply because your ego is invested in your likes and dislikes.

Life can be enhanced when you free yourself from your likes and dislikes and especially your labels.

COMMANDMENT 9

Thou Shalt Have Wonder

"In praise and blame, always the same"
Satya Sai Baba

"Verily I say unto you, unless ye be converted and become as little children, ye shall not enter into the kingdom of heaven"
Matthew 18

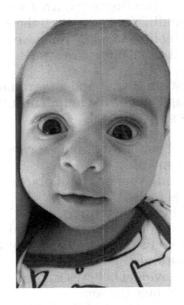

Wonderful—full of wonder.

Wonder defined: miracle, be in awe, phenomenon, sensation, amazing thing, and awesome sight, spectacle, seeing the beauty, grace, and majesty in all things.

Many towns in New Jersey have their local fire departments conduct July 4th fireworks displays. In July of 1998, I loaded up the car with my family and my mother, who at the time was in her late 70s. We situated ourselves in a large field close to the action. With blankets, chairs, and insect repellent, we waited patiently for the show to begin. As the early summer sun finally set, the first explosions signaled the beginning of the half hour display. Amidst the cheers and applause, I heard deep sighs, gasps, and ooo's from my mother sitting next to me. She was so animated; I became concerned for her health. Immediately I asked if she was O.K. She turned to me reassuringly, smiled and then turned her attention back to the loud, explosive light show of colors. After the tumultuous finale, my mother beaming with enthusiasm, turned to us and exclaimed how inspirational the display was for her. With the excitement and wonder of a child, she said "You know, I have never seen a live firework display before". I thought to myself, how extraordinary, a woman of her age never having seen live fireworks. What was amazing, though, was my mother's childlike reaction. With the wonder of a child, mom exhibited the biblical saying, "You have to become like a little child to enter the kingdom of heaven".

The difference between a saint and an ordinary person is that a saint can create magic out of the mundane and find the lessons in all circumstances.

That's the mental power that can heal cancer or make something extraordinary manifest.

Inviting wonder into your spiritual practice is a viable, powerful, transformational tool.

You might have heard the term "beginner's mind".

It is a metaphor for being open to new and fresh teachings.

If an individual keeps this attitude of emptiness, the hunger for learning stays natural.

As soon as an individual believes in their own expertise and knowing, learning becomes slower.

When you are at the bottom of the mountain, you can keep growing and climbing. The only way is up.

When you are at the pinnacle of the mountain, when you think you know all there is, the only way is down the other side.

Learning, like climbing, continues when you are childlike.

Shunryu Suzuki states:
"If your mind is empty,
It is always ready for anything.
It is open to anything.
In the beginner's mind there are many possibilities.
In the expert's mind there are few."

"If you keep your original mind,

The precepts will keep themselves.
In the beginner's mind there is no thought,
'I have attained something.'
All self-centered thoughts limit our vast mind.
When we have no thought of achievement,
No thought of self,
We are true beginners."

Hilda possessed a beginner's mind mixed with childlike enthusiasm.

In fact, it was one of her spiritual secrets.

She could turn the most mundane of events into an extraordinary learning experience.

Finding the wonder and magic in the smallest of life's experiences.

One evening Hilda gathered a bunch of us together and announced, "We are going to the movies".

This was rare because Hilda believed what you put into your consciousness mentally should be as healthy as what you put into your body. All input was food and to support your spiritual development, it should be of the highest quality. Most movies are about entertainment and just clog up your subconscious with melodrama. She would say, "On the spiritual path, kids, you must keep good company". She was, however, excited about a new movie that was playing about Noah's Ark. She exclaimed, "How extraordinary the circumstances were, when God was ready to lay waste to the Earth, he gave advanced notice to Noah". She wanted us to have the personal relationship with God, along with the intuition of a Noah. In this way, we would have an advanced warning system for whatever would befall the fate of our own lives. A master soul must be eternally vigilant and listen to their inner voice. Hilda said while everyone was partying, Noah was paying attention and prepared.

So, we went to the show, and I got to sit next to Hilda.

I knew that was trouble. Hilda read people's minds. It was crazy, her ability.

Here I am, an opinionated pseudo-intellectual with a monkey mind, sitting next to a gifted, highly psychic meditation master.

All the while, watching what must be one of the worst movies of all time. The movie was part documentary, and the host was a Ph. D with a bad hairpiece. His toupee bounced whenever he got emphatic with his words.

"Noah talked to God!"
Toupee... Bounce, bounce, bounce, bounce!

When we were leaving the theater, Hilda turned to me and
with a shakti-filled bang on my chest, exclaimed...
"Wasn't that fabulous, kid?"
Hilda's powers were such that a simple bang could keep one
from sleeping for 24 hours.
She was a reservoir of spiritual power.
With her bang on my chest, my mind went up like an
infield fly.
I had lost whatever objectivity I once possessed.
"Think of the miracle of Noah, kid, not the quality of the
movie".
She was into the concept, when life gives you lemons, make
lemonade (or so I thought).
Turns out it was not about the movie at all.
It was about the company I was keeping and the lessons I
would receive.
See the wonder of all phenomena and you will consistently be
ahead of the game.
What is more, you will never waste a precious second of your
life.
It was perhaps the worst movie of all time, with one of the
best personal lessons for me.
And here I am writing about it many, years later.

Hilda was fond of a story about Swami Paramahansa
Yogananda, the incredible yogi saint who authored the best-
seller, *Autobiography of a Yogi*.
Swamiji, as she fondly called him, was always in and out of
states of spiritual ecstasy.
One day Swami asked the young Hilda to accompany him
into his kitchen. Swami's excitement was infectious, and Hilda
believed "this is it". This enlightened being was about to transmit
a great teaching, perhaps open the ancient archives known as the
Akashic Records. As she entered the room, Swamiji was standing
by the sink. His smile and twinkling eyes invited her closer. She
thought, oh, Swamiji is going to transfer a great dispensation of
Spirit, what they call in India Shakti-pat. The transmission of a
teacher's power.
Instead, he took a carrot from the cupboard, put it in a hole in
the sink, pressed a button and poof...the carrot disappeared.

Laughing with great ardor, Swami introduced Hilda to this invention called a garbage disposal.

The young Hilda left the room scratching her head in wonderment.

So much for the Divine dispensation.

Later in her life, Hilda realized this great God man's simplicity and wonder is what fueled his Divinity and contributed to his enlightenment.

Every experience is an opportunity, a lesson; every person might be your teacher, your guide. Pay attention to the omens. Everywhere you are sent, you are sent to help, to teach, to learn.

Find the teachings in all things, become like a child, and see magic afoot in all things. Remember, the Universe is interactive. Hilda said, "We'll take what we get, and we'll make what we want."

COMMANDMENT 10

Thou Shalt Have Fervor!

"God spews out of his mouth the lukewarm."
Revelation 3-16

Fervor defined:
passion, enthusiasm, dedication, eagerness, zeal, commitment, vehemence, ardor, excitement

Near the end of her life, Hilda was hospitalized at Dover General Hospital in New Jersey.

Her condition was considered very serious. Her personal physician was my best friend, Dr. Wally.

There was a buzz throughout the hospital about this great healer and teacher.

Physicians and nurses alike came to meet her and read her chart.

The attending cardiologist was shocked by the results of his tests.

He took Dr. Wally aside and exclaimed that, *"Hilda's actual heart tissue has atrophied.*

Her heart size is one quarter of what it should be.

So severe. Should she be in a wheelchair?"

Dr. Wally smiled and told him perhaps for a normal individual that would be the case.

Hilda, however, was no normal individual.

This was a woman who had lived her entire life devoted to intensive meditation and spiritual practice.

Hilda had taught a class at St. John the Divine Cathedral just two nights ago for over five hundred people and recently returned from a world spiritual pilgrimage with a group of her students.

Hilda lived by different rules. Most great ones do. Her divine mind and spiritual fervor were quite capable of taking over where her body could not. To have fervor is to be marked by great intensity of feeling.

To be passionate, fiery, and ardent.

Hilda embraced fervor as part of her spiritual practice and teaching.

She taught her students to be excited about even the smallest of things.

To her it was better to be "hell bent for heaven" than a wishy-washy namby-pamby.

Hilda defined a spiritual slacker as one who possessed a sloppy, lazy mind, filled with poor concentration, with weak powers of observation, that gets easily sidetracked.

She cajoled her students to see everything tinged with Spirit and possibility.

To see the magic of Spirit or the hand of God in all our life's eddies and floes.

There could be no mundane experiences because every event in our life was purposely put here for our own development and evolution.

Every event is an opportunity for us to get the lessons and move on.

To Hilda, the entire Universe was in on our quest toward liberation and the blueprint of enlightenment, the spark of Divinity, was alive in all things. CAN YOU SAY INTERACTIVE UNIVERSE?

Hilda whole-heartedly believed that if you could perform sleight of hand with your mind, you could turn your entire world into a wonderfully amazing experience.

It's the "renew yourself by the renewing of your mind" concept.

We were hanging out with Hilda in her living room one Sunday afternoon.

Hilda was talking to us about crystals.

She was telling us how everyone seemed to be into healing stones.

"They say these quartz crystals can transmit and store the secrets of the Universe," Hilda quipped. *"When programmed with your mind, they can transmit a power that can be used in healing."* Then she announced, *"It's time to have some fun. Larry; please stand up."*

Of course, as fate would have it, this was the first time I was invited to Hilda's house.

So, I knew I was going to be the lesson of the day.

Like fresh meat ready for the ego-ectomy.

I hesitantly rose, dumb smile on my face.

Hilda said, *"Now let's see how psychic he is, kids. OK, stand firm, pull into your center, close your eyes, now feel for a second and tell me where the crystal is.*

Hilda waved the large clear quartz in a circle around my head.

I felt it with my eyes closed.

"Where is it?" she queried me.

I immediately pointed to my head area.

She said, *"Good, open your eyes".*

With her big smile of approval, Hilda's hand was still three feet in front of my face.

She patted me on the shoulder and said, *"Let's try again; close your eyes".*

This time she made a big circle around the middle of my body and again I felt the energy and guessed correctly.

This time she gave me a nod of approval. As if to say, not bad.

The third and last test turned out completely different.

This time I felt an incredible force around my chest and then *bang*, a small explosion!

It felt like Hilda had smacked me on the chest.

Her energy moved me from my spot without her physically touching me.

Then I felt a rush of Love, like when she hugged me the first time we met.

I startled, flung my eyes open, to find Hilda with a huge smile, one hand in the air as if being sworn in by a judge.

Mischievously she sung out, "NO CRYSTAL!"

This pastel was lovingly created by my dear friend and colleague
Louise Mahoney, LMT.

Hilda taught her students to make "a quick adjustment of mind".

For me it was more like "an instant shock of God awakening". Hilda turned to the crowded living room, *"Kids", she said, "You don't need any props like these crystals in this world".*
Learn how to use your God-given powers.
Believe beyond a shadow of a doubt in God's ability to work through you."
Hilda's *fervor* had filled the room.
The energy was thick and tangible, like an influence tugging at your heart.
We all sat there feeling Hilda open the door to our hearts.
You can feel it now. Breathe this Love into your heart center, fill yourself with Divinity,
let a smile come to your lips. Now breathe Light out to the world. Wherever you think Light is needed.

Last story about having **fervor**.

When the Nazis realized the war was lost, they abandoned the concentration camps.

Leaving the surviving prisoners locked in without food for weeks. When the allies liberated the camps, they questioned the remaining survivors. They wanted to know how they had managed to stay alive in these final days, frail, weakened, and without the barest of provisions. One of the victims said, when the food ran out, those that believed they were starving to death simply died. We all knew the allies were close, so we decided we were not going to be starved. Instead, we decided it was in our power to fast.

The simple twist, victim to empowered, saved their life.

You too, can turn being a victim into victory.

NO MORE VICTIM MENTALITY.

As you strengthen your mind, you cut through life's melodrama. Slice the darkness with your higher resolve. Put your power behind your heart and mind's direction. Breathe and create an impeccable force.

You are being trained to perform a Nasa Mission. This is the Nasa Mission of life. STEP UP...

COMMANDMENT 11

Thou Shalt Be Generous

"And if any man will sue thee at the law, and take away thy coat,
let him have thy cloak also".
Mathew 5:40, King James Version

Saint Therese, Little Flower said,
"I want to spend my heaven in doing good on Earth, it is a great
mistake to worry about what trouble there may be in store.
It is like meddling in God's work. We who walk in the way of
love must never allow ourselves to be disturbed by anything."

Little flower also said, **"Walk in my path and your path**
shall be strewn with rose petals as mine was."

Hilda never charged for her classes.
She was economically poor and with the hundreds and
thousands of folks she sincerely touched, she could have
made a substantial living. I always thought she was rich. Her
unquenchable desire for liberation and her goodness personified
was beautiful and courageous. She sincerely believed that
spiritual teachings should flow freely and unconditionally to all.
That is one of the things that made her great and memorable. She
would give it away with a completely open heart. In essence, she
was saying, *"Imagine if Jesus took up a collection or charged an*
admission before he would administer his Sermon on the Mount."

Generosity comes from the heart and improves the lives of us
all profoundly.
And let us be crystal clear about this.

Generosity on our part ultimately benefits us.

I want everyone around me to be as smart, as healthy, as creative, and as enlightened as humanly possible and if I could do things to make that happen faster, Amen to that. That is how you get into heaven!

Philanthropists are revered for their unconditional generosity.

Their acts of selflessness and sacrifice for the common good of all is considered Christ-like.

We honor them, construct edifices and foundations in their names.

Others, however, have the expectation that when giving a gift of time, wisdom or money, there should be something coming back in return—an exchange, a give and take. They call it "quid pro quo". It goes along with that eye-for-an eye mentality. If your generosity comes with conditions, that's obviously not unconditional love; that is a form of emotional capitalism. The conditions could be minor. It might just be that getting good grades, or a haircut is all that is required to receive this gift. But it's still doled out with conditions. So that is partially love and partially a barter arrangement. I'll show you love and attention if you _____ (fill in the expectation).

Sorry, but whenever you withhold love and genuine kindness to gain control over someone, that manipulative behavior is small and weak. In the end, you will really regret not being more generous.

Generosity is not just about money, but for many of you it is.

Also, be generous with your patience, with your time, with your wisdom, gifts, talents, emotional support, compliments, and especially your love.

Start today. Give from your heart fully and deeply.

Generosity is about giving from your heart unconditionally.

My teacher, Michio Kushi, in his thoughtfully spoken broken English, once grabbed me in the hallway before class, all the while tapping me with his finger on my heart center, he said the following, lovingly...

> **"Larry, give it all away...**
> **the more you give away,**

the richer you'll become."

One of the Native American teachings is to be invisible, to walk humbly, quietly, anonymously through the world, and yet to change it profoundly. There are so many great people that have done this, but you will never know who they are because they are the invisible architects of our human evolution. Hilda used to say that if you get the credit for something down here, you won't get credit for it upstairs. But... if you do it without ego, without the need for credit, that is greatness that will be part of you forever.

So be generous with your compliments, with your open heart, with your listening ear and healing energy, wisdom, compassion, a helping hand, a prayer, patience, or a tangible, material item. Be generous and let it flow through you like Ram Dass' guru used to say, "FEED PEOPLE."

We have already established that service is half of our life prime directive (Commandment 2). If what you reap is what you sow, and every action has an equal and opposite reaction, then we are just talking self-preservation. *"What you do to the least of my brethren, that you do unto me."*

The secret of friendship is to extend a hand, be a friend.
The secret of love is to give love.
The secret of healing yourself is to help heal others.

Thou Shalt Be Generous because, *"As you love, you are doubly blessed, for it flows through you first and then touches the beloved."*
Hilda

COMMANDMENT 12

Thou Shalt Strive for Excellence

Don't be a lukewarm, namby-pamby.
Be sincere. Make believe you are trying to save a life.
Step Up!

Put your heart and soul into your learning, projects, assignments,
and day-to-day life.
Give it your all! Don't do sloppy work.

We are on a planet where everyone is pretty much a beginner.
To fulfill the prime directive,
"To grow in every way you can and to uplift, inspire, and
serve wherever you may go.
Excellence should be part of your daily conditioning.
It's a spiritual thing.
It can speed up the process.
Would you rather have a good surgeon or an excellent sur-
geon? A good football team or an excellent one?
If you are ever to fulfill your destiny in this life, you need to
step up.
Those of us still struggling with the ego's lower traps and at-
tachments, insecurities, and inferiority complexes—lifetime after
lifetime—will continue like a rat on a wheel, destined to take the
course repeatedly.
Those folks that permeate wisdom and mastery,
extraordinary talent and energy, are just old souls that have
probably done this earth thing quite a number of times and are
finally getting really good at it. They are the Saints amongst us.
None the less, there is an expiration date on YOU and your clock
is ticking.
That is why I've been such a bug about eating a plant-based
diet, taking supplements, alkalizing your bloodstream, and
especially keeping your body young and flexible.
Your hunger to grow will increase and the pain of separation
from your higher self will become greater and greater until it
becomes all encompassing.

NOW WE ARE GOING TO MAKE IT EASIER...

First notice the wording. It specifically says,

"Strive for excellence."

The word strive means to do your best; that does give us some room to maneuver.

You do not have to live up to any other person's definition of excellence, **just your own.**

You do not need anyone really to point out your inequities, just honestly look in the mirror and your work will be in front of you.

Excellence is your ally because it is a strategy you will use to continually excel in everything and anything.

Just go back to the drawing board, IDENTIFY WHERE YOU MIGHT HAVE COME UP SHORT, visualize in your mind's eye yourself DOING IT OVER THIS TIME.

Just try to improve, if only to hold your center and not allow someone to press your buttons.

Maybe to find the will to skip dessert or control a negative brain.

Eventually, with enough honest self-reflection and practice, excellence will be within your reach.

Joseph Campbell was best known for his work in comparative mythology. Although he passed on in 1987, it was not until the following year that Bill Moyers on PBS introduced the world to this amazing man and his teachings.

When queried by Moyers as to **"how to know what your true work is?"**, Campbell responded by saying,

"Follow your bliss".

You have probably seen this adage on a bumper sticker. Campbell's explanation was simple. Identify the things in life you really love. Then find a way to work in what you love. Because of the greater interest and enjoyment, you will be more motivated and achieve at a higher level of excellence. Your vocation (the way you earn a living) and your avocation (the way you fulfill your spirit) will be one and the same.

So, for starters **let your skills, talents, and loves influence and identify your work for you.**

You know, make a list, brainstorm with some friend or loved ones, pick the brain of someone who works in that field, but figure it out. You need to put some real passion and elbow grease behind it. Then remember the words of the great and wise Chinese Book of Changes called the I Ching,

"Perseverance furthers one to cross the great water".

And the age-old New York advice... Question: "How do I get to Carnegie Hall?"

Answer: "Practice, practice, practice!"

Dialogue with yourself constantly and psyche yourself up to achieve at this higher level. Like a baseball player attempting to lay off a bad pitch, you must talk and even scream at yourself sometimes, "Stay away from the high, outside pitch!" In our case it will be about no negative self-talk, no gossip, and no sitting in judgment. Use positive affirmations to re-program your subconscious from the negative inner dialogue that we all seem to carry around from our early programming.

And remember the words of St. Theresa, **"We who walk in the way of love must never allow ourselves to be disturbed by anything."** So, let's modify that advice a bit, shall we?

We who walk in the way of excellence must never surrender to our lower ego or challenged nature; nor should we allow ourselves to be seized by the outside negative forces afoot.

If you never allowed yourself to be disturbed (controlled) by anything, you would be a total Master Soul.

Good luck with that.

The negative forces out there would like nothing more than to keep you from coming into your power.

So, when you fail or when you fall, which is inevitable at times, simply lift yourself up, dust yourself off, and walk on!

My friend, Office Manager and wise woman Kathleen Moran, lays out the formula for you to achieve your dreams and fulfill your destiny. She personally guarantees that it will work. I, for one, completely believe her.

- Write down specifically what you want.
- Visualize or picture it clearly.
- Visualize your ultimate intention for the highest good.
- **Feel it deeply** and **fuel it with your emotions**. Be there with it.
- Picture the outcome.
- Feel great gratitude.
- Do this daily.

It is excellence that fuels our personal evolution.

COMMANDMENT 13

Thou Shalt Have Rhythm

"Riga mortise sets in way before you die."
Larry Heisler

One of the secrets of spiritual life is to have a body that is rhythmic, open, and flexible.

This assures us of a body system that can carry a strong vibrant charge, which in turn will support your vision and spiritual intentions.

If you have a body like this, you are one step closer to achieving your spiritual vision. Live right and you will attain it.

For the rest of us who were not born with the gift of rhythm, it will happen in time. Just follow the lifestyle recommendations in this book and you will find your rhythm.

To understand how the energy flows through our body, we look to one of the oldest approaches practiced in the world, Acupuncture Medicine.

Acupuncture sometimes refers to the human electro-magnetic system as simply the **energetic system**. It's the internal electrical engineering template of the human body.

The terms *bio-electric or electromagnetic current* can also be interchanged. Both electrical and magnetic impulses enter our spine, innervating our entire being with their minute charges.

The macrobiotic paradigm refers to the source where the electrical charges come from: the heavens, and in particular, our Milky Way galaxy. The electrical impulses enter in through the spirals on the top of our heads. These spirals are called whorls.

This is how spirals work.

A man's spiral moves in a clock-wise direction and a woman's spiral moves in a counterclockwise direction.

The human magnetic charge origi-nates from the Earth's molten iron core as it rotates, creating magnetic

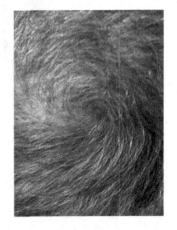

charge. These magnetic impulses rise up from the earth and enter the human body at the perineum, located between the reproductive organs and anus. As the magnetic impulses continue to rise up the spine, electrical impulses descend along the same spine. The two forces then implode, creating a highly charged internal atmosphere.

These two charges, electrical and magnetic, heaven and earth, activate the spine, charging the internal organ structures and streaming out just under the surface of the skin to the hands and feet.

Our body carries these minute bio-electric charges along twelve energy pathways called meridians and two major vessels called the *Conception* and *Governing vessels*.

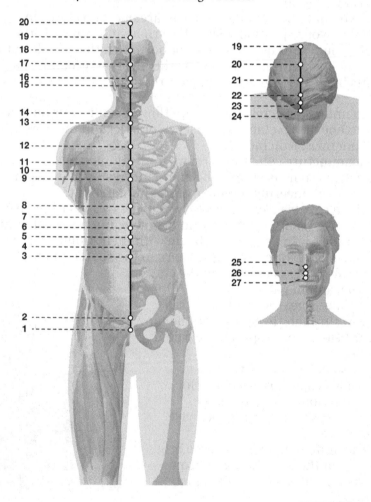

The vessels that run along the center front of our body (anteriorly) are called the *Conception* Vessel.

The vessels that run along the center back of our body (posteriorly) are called the *Governing* Vessel.

On an acupuncture chart, they look like a New York City subway map.

Along these 12 meridians, there are about 365 acupuncture points on each side of our body. These acupuncture points are commonly referred to as "tsubos" in Japanese. These tsubos are used to gain access into the energetic flow, treat specific conditions, and affect change in our bodies' functioning.

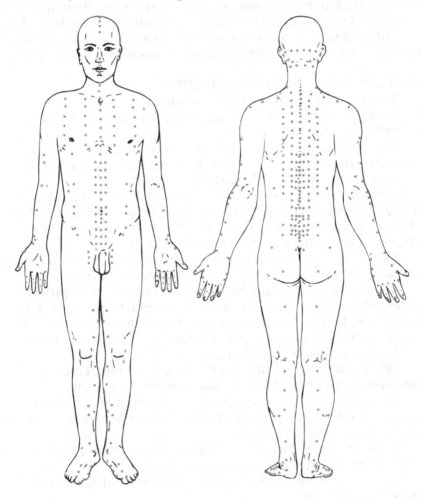

The energy that flows through our body is called *Chi* in China, *Ki* in Japan, *Gi* in Korea, *prana* in India, *Pneuma* in Greece, and *Ruach* in Hebrew. Freud's famous student, Dr. Wilhelm Reich (sometimes called the father of bioenergetics), referred to the energy that flows through our body as **Orgone** energy. Western thought refers to this energy as the electromagnetic flow of our body. Others refer to it as *spirit or life-force.*

Until very recently, western medical thinking did not pay much attention to this energetic way of looking at the body. In fact, they were suspicious and disdainful of the Eastern energetic concept.

However, now that we have sophisticated electrical instrumentation, infra-red photography, and radioactive dyes, these lines, points, and vessels have been clearly delineated and confirmed.

This is amazing when you consider that the original acupuncture charts were accurately portrayed thousands of years ago.

HERE'S WHY YOU JUST LEARNED THIS

This is our internal electrical engineering.

When one is healthy, they have an open, flowing, and balanced energetic system.

You can confirm this by their ease of movement, natural flexibility, warm, soft muscles, and a smooth, even way of expression.

Even their words are flowing and smooth.

When we stand, our spine is electromagnetically charged like a human acupuncture needle, receiving and transmitting this bio-electric charge from the galaxy or earth center and sending it up and down our spine and throughout our body.

This is also why we sit upright when meditating. When you lie down to rest or sleep, it cuts off the bio-electric charge.

To achieve this flowing body, which enhances our **spiritual potential**, we must break up our body's energetic stagnation. By stagnation, I mean blockages and poor circulation. These can be caused by hardness, pain, and imbalances in the energy flow.

It is a big task, but we chip away at it little by little.

My teachers taught me that dis-ease is an imbalance or blockage in an individual's personal energetic system.

Thus, our internal organs, their meridian lines, and their specific acupuncture points can all become compromised and start affecting our whole person.

Also, in this philosophy of healing, there is no separation between the body, mind, emotions, or Spirit.

When we say, "whole person", we are not just talking about a person's soft tissue.

If there is a problem with any one system, all body systems can be affected.

For example, in Japanese the word for *anger* is "Kan Shaku", which translates as, *liver disease.*

So, if you go to your family physician and exclaim that you have been "harboring a lot of anger lately, doc," the physician's response may include a prescription for an anti-depressive/anxiety type drug and perhaps a referral to a therapist so you may discuss some of your issues.

It might not be a bad solution, but if you go to a macrobiotic or integrative doctor or counselor, you would likely be taken off all foods that they believe overwork the liver (saturated fats, eggs, chemical exposure, over-eating, alcohol, OTC drugs).

In a couple of weeks, your anger might have dissipated, and the problem would be solved without long-term therapy or drugs with potential side effects.

My point is, all your health inequities and issues directly affect your spirit, your mind, and your emotions.

There is NO SEPARATION between your Spirit, your mind, and your emotions; you are a complete being, not a body that is separate from its other parts.

If you are interested in discovering more about the relationship between food, internal organs, and how it affects the aging of your body, please refer to my book, **Soft Tissue Revolution.** www.softtissuerevolution.net also available on Amazon and Barnes and Nobles

Soft Tissue Revolution
The New Bodywork Paradigm

Larry Heisler, MA, LMT

"I love this book.... thank you so much for doing this!
Should be in every therapist's library for quick reference!
And it should be in EVERY massage school!"

Mike Hinkle, Founder of the World Massage Festival and Massage Therapy Hall of Fame

So, if "Thou shalt have rhythm," is true, how do you find your innate, rhythmic flow?

How we move, how we flow, gives us an indication of how young we are and sometimes even how much Spirit we possess.

But as we age, our bodies become dynamically more rigid and shrink in stature.

The muscles shorten, causing you to lose flexibility. The body tends to become hard and tight with many cold and poorly circulating parts.

In the Orient, rigidity, hardness, and cold spots on the body indicate stagnation.

If you run your hand over your body, every cold spot indicates an imbalance.

The belief is, if an area has poor circulation over a long period of time, there is a tendency toward degenerating health, particularly for the organs in that area.

A cold butt can indicate poor circulation in the pelvic region. If it stays like that for years, it can be a significant indicator of future reproductive problems.

Thus, **our flexibility is an indicator of our youthfulness, and aging can be defined by one's hardness.**

In a sense, rigor mortis, the stiffening that takes place when something dies, begins to set in way before your end.

Let me say that again,

"Rigor mortis sets in way before you die."

With my massage clients, I have always looked at hardness as a warning sign.

Remember, **hardness very often can mean more than poor circulation; it can also be an indicator of oxygen deprivation and an acidic blood condition.**

Here is another way to look at it.

In the 1930s, Dr. Otto Warburg, a medical doctor and research scientist (often referred to as the greatest biochemist of the 20th century), won the Nobel Prize for showing that a 35% decrease in bodily oxygen resulted in the body's cells creating cancer.

At that time, medical researchers knew that oxygen deprivation led to cancer, but they did not know how to increase the oxygen supply in our body.

Now we know of many ways to do so.

In the 1970s, if you asked a cardiologist if there was any food to eat, supplement to take, or technique to use that would address your heart condition, the routine answer might be,

"No, heart disease is genetic. The best we can do is manage your symptoms with prescription medications".

That was the answer that most medical practitioners would give, whether the question was in regard to heart disease, arthritis, asthma, multiple sclerosis, or something else.

When questioned further about a diet like macrobiotics or Pritikin, they would use the "Q" word.

QUAKERY!

So, prescription drugs were the cat's meow, and vitamins, well, they made expensive urine. Dietary regimens to address serious medical conditions were seriously frowned upon as dangerous fads. Herbs were laughable, acupuncture and Oriental medicine was weird voodoo. At the time, hospital dieticians were the only respected nutritional experts. In reality, genetics, stress, smoking, and obesity were and still are the cause of many such conditions. However, there was at the time major resistance to change within the medical profession.

Then Nathan Pritikin came along...

When Dr. Pritikin was in residence at the famed Mayo Clinic (early 1980s), he was doing things that had never been done before, dramatically healing what was considered at that time to be incurable, degenerative diseases. This included everything from congestive heart failure and rheumatoid arthritis to insulin-dependent diabetes and heart disease in all its forms.

In one study, Dr. Pritikin took a group of men confined to wheelchairs, all in their early sixties.

In these men, blood supply to the legs was so compromised that the average guy could only walk a couple hundred feet before being placed back into their wheelchair.

There were two groups in Dr. Pritikin's study. The control group was asked to follow the American Heart Association's dietary recommendations, and the experimental group was asked to follow a very low fat, high complex-carbohydrate diet.

They called it the "Pritikin" diet back then, but today we would call it the Mediterranean diet.

Dr. Pritikin's New York Times best-sellers were titled *The Pritikin Program for Diet and Exercise and Live Longer Now*. His diet was predominately one that was rich in whole cereal grains like brown rice, barley, quinoa, millet, and oatmeal. It also included a significant amount of beans, soups, and salads, leafy green vegetables. The diet recommended only small, supplemental amounts of lean animal proteins such as fish and white meat poultry. In other words, meat was the side dish rather than the main course.

He recommended that dieters never consume more than three ounces of flesh foods in any given day.

It was an extremely strict diet. No simple carbohydrates like white bread, bagels, muffins, white rice, noodles, desserts, sugar, alcohol, or junk food were allowed. Also, every man in the study agreed to walk throughout the day.

BUT remember..., these guys were allegedly at the end of their lives. It was a very bleak situation.

Living in a wheelchair, not being able to walk with their grandchild, dance with the love of their life, play a sport, or even make love. Nada.

Within six months, on this low fat, no junk food, **plant-based diet**, the results were **so dramatic as to be almost unbelievable. Knock, knock!**

Every guy in the program was walking six to ten miles a day, most of them began jogging before the program concluded.

Say that again Larry...most were *jogging*!

The seemingly incurable, irreversible conditions, at least according to the modern medicine of the time, were all reversed! When questioned about the amazing, somewhat miraculous results, Dr. Pritikin carefully explained that with a regular exercise routine, the predominately plant-based regimen would alkalize the bloodstream, raising the oxygen content of the blood within a few weeks.

The improved circulation quickly improved his patients' conditions and permitted their bodies to start the healing process.

This was the key to their permanent recovery.

Pritikin explained that the dramatic effectiveness of his regimen was due to the combination of the high fiber/extremely low-fat plant-based diet, along with daily exercise. The combination produced a significant increase in blood flow and oxygen levels in the blood. The improved circulation quickly influenced the patient's condition for the better and jumped started their body's healing process and recovery!

The diet that Pritikin used in his study resembled the diets of populations all over the world which have the lowest incidence of degenerative disease. Dr. Ancel Keys of the Framingham Institute in Massachusetts has conducted the most worldwide epidemiological studies in which the relationship between diet and disease was investigated. After a lifetime of research, **Dr. Keys has not found a single exception to the general rule correlating the high complex carb, low-fat regimen with a lower incidence of disease in every population he studied worldwide.**

Clearly our lifestyle choices (meditation, diet, beverages, supplements, exercise) **play a major role.**
So here are some guidelines for finding your rhythm and fulfilling this commandment. It has been my experience that when a person transitions to a healthy, grain oriented, plant-based diet and adds the exercise and other lifestyle changes previously described, sometime within the first five years they find their rhythm. The exact time period differs by case.
But what's remarkable is that all of sudden the person begins to move more freely and smoothly.

1. Eat low on the food chain. Wherever you go in the world, the more animal products you consume, the more disease you get. The less animal products you consume, the less disease you get.
    It's that simple.
    Besides, the animal killing industry uses up the worlds resources at an alarming rate, all for money, i.e., the world's resources used in the production of livestock for consumption:
    · **33%** of world's fish catch [30]
    · **38%** of the world's grain harvest [31]
    · **50%** of all the water used in the US [32]
    · **60%** of Brazil's grain harvest [33]
    · **70%** of US grain harvest [34]
    · **80%** of US corn harvest [35]
    · **Almost half** of all energy expended in US agriculture [36]
Check the references at www.earthsave.org/environmental.htm.

2. **What you consume directly affects your body and mind.**
    Remember, food turns into blood, blood turns into cells, and cells make up every aspect of your body and the human experience. Poor, inadequate nutrition creates a catastrophic body and mind from the cells on up.

3. **When you are healthy and consume more than your body can burn as fuel,** the excess will result in some form of discharge. Medicine calls the body's natural correction to the excess a sickness and tries to quell the symptoms with prescription and over-the-counter drugs. When the body is not strong enough to produce an outward detox, the excess begins to accumulate internally, and the degenerative process begins to take hold. This was what I learned from my Japanese macrobiotic teachers.

4. **A flexible, healthy body is alkaline and flush with abundant stores of oxygen.** An acid body is depleted of oxygen and is host to an abundance of maladies and misfortunes. Aside from negative emotions, the most acid-forming foods are animal foods, sugar, soda, coffee, and simple carbohydrates.

5. **Nutrition is the single most powerful choice.** Eating food that is unprocessed, organic, local, and in-season can be vitally important. If it's been made for you, for your convenience, chances are it's been altered, over salted, over sweetened, over chemicalized. Stick to the complex carbohydrates like whole grains and beans, seeds, nuts, soups, salads, fruits, veggies, and lots of leafy green vegetables. Fermented soy products like miso, tempeh, and tamari are also exceptional alkaline and probiotic sources of nutrition and sea vegetation (seaweeds) are abundant in hard-to-get minerals. Use really good quality whole salt for the trace minerals. Expect the better, mineral rich salt to be much more expensive. Stick with alkaline beverage sources of water. Remember, the better the, fuel the more efficient your vehicle will run. And don't forget to take your vitamins; they really help and will add years onto your life!

6. **The best exercises** for spiritual development are the ones that focus on opening up the energetic system (meridians). Breaking up the hardness, cold, and stagnation in one's body, balances the energetic system, improves circulation, and increases oxygen levels. It also promotes physical suppleness and encourages long life. With a strong, steady chi, the individual tends to have an increasing connection and sensitivity to the spirit in everything. Massage, yoga, tai chi, Pilates, and chi kung exercise all contribute to this greater fluidity, supporting a greater ability to summon

up your personal power (chi) when needed. All exercise is beneficial and the ones who keep their meridian systems open will extend their shelf life with quality.

7. Upon reaching their hundredth birthdays, Bob Hope, George Burns, and Rose Kennedy were queried for **the secret of their longevity.** Each of them said **daily deep tissue massage** was the key. Massage breaks up the hardness of aging. While it might seem costly to get a daily massage session, adding years onto one's life in such an effortless, enjoyable way is certainly something that can be added to the spiritual equation. For most of us, an occasional deep tissue session will do wonders as well. It will keep you young and dancing late into your senior years.

8. **Daily meditation** will significantly add to your personal chi. People who meditate daily get sick less frequently, deal with stress more efficiently, and develop an abundance of personal energy and self-control.

It is easy to know who you were in a past life or to study the secret spiritual and esoteric arts. It is much, much, harder to do and live the basics—eating really well daily and chewing your food thoroughly, meditating and exercising regularly, consistently remembering to take your vitamins, staying positive and not allowing other folks to decide how you feel. So, when the winds of adversity hit, it is the basics of life that set your foundation in bedrock and help you hold your center. Within a few years, your body will begin to shed its hardness, developing a smoother, more rhythmic you. You will move with a greater grace and fluidity. In this instance, rhythm is a serious sign of health.

Here's a question for you.

How can a lifestyle that promotes cancer, ill health, and degenerative disease promote personal growth towards enlightenment? Ask your minister.

"And God said, Behold, I have given you every herb baring seed, which is upon the face of all the earth, and every tree, in the which is the fruit of a yielding seed tree: to you it shall be for meat.
Genesis 1:29 (KJV)

How to Use this Information

You are here to grow and to serve.
That's Prime.
To live a life that is filled with enlightened choices, both joyful and creative.
A life, you can say, that has fulfilled your destiny.
To make a difference.
To come fully into your power and love.
As you re-read the Commandments and make them part of your daily thoughts, the provocative spiritual ideas herein will begin to replace your lifetime of conditioning, whining and insecurity.
Don't get frustrated.
Everyone battles their ego demons.
Remember how you get to Carnegie Hall...practice.
You are going to fail sometimes and drop the ball.
Remember, we are all Bozos on this bus.
Just visualize the scene in your head and see yourself saying the correct words, performing the right actions.
Try to have a sense of humor.
As your inner voice becomes more prominent, you will know what is true and what is not.
There is a big difference between spirituality and religion.
The most difficult path to walk is filled with the daily basics, even for ministers and religious leaders.
It's easy to quote scripture, along with esoteric knowledge.
It's really challenging to eat a healthy plant-based diet, chew each mouthful really well, remember to take your vitamins every day, be consistent with your exercise, your prayers, your daily meditation, to avoid giving your power away and playing the victim, stand tall, consistently uplift and inspire others, and most importantly, **love, grow, and serve**.
This is what walking the walk is all about.
Like I said, the walk is spiritual, not necessarily religious.
Also, when you take one step toward the Masters, they will take ten steps towards you—quietly, silently, secretly, to support you on your spiritual journey..
If you pay supreme attention, you might see or feel the inner world.
On those days that the spiritual path is the most difficult, challenge imaginable, remember, the path of enlightenment is easy for those who have flush toilets and air conditioners.
You still are going to have to Step Up!
Sometimes waaaay up!

And every time you do, your Light uplifts the world!
For the children on the planet.
For all of us.

One more thought...
You can **do** this!

How do you know you are not free?
You feed your ego, your lower self, as you react negatively.
You get angry, impatient, jealous, whiny, and fearful when you
don't get your way.
As you strengthen your mind,
you'll cut through life's melodrama,
slice the darkness with your higher resolve,
put your power behind your heart and mind and create a force.
And this force can change your world and the world around you.
DO IT.
Live IT.
You got the power!
Believe!

Finally, ... A Miraculous Story
One that perfectly illustrates the entire point of this book.

My mother passed away in 2010.
When she was alive, she routinely displayed intuitive gifts and powers.
She often knew when people were going to die, and she saved neighbors and strangers lives on multiple occasions which I witnessed personally five times.
I've had mediums and psychics talk about mom with great reverence and accolade.
When I got married in 2014, mom showed up at the wedding.
I'll tell you the story.
The ceremony was completed, as well as the first dance, the speeches and the toast.
As we were just settling down to eat a little, a waitress approached the bridal table and said, "That was the most beautiful wedding I have ever attended, if there is anything that you need, I will be available, just ask for Esther.
After she left, I turned to my new wife Kathy and exclaimed, *"How sweet and she had my mother's name to boot."*
The rest of the story I didn't know about until the next day.
My daughter Ariella called and said,
"Dad did you meet a waitress at the wedding who introduced herself as Esther?"
I said *"yes, she came over to the bridal table to tell us how beautiful and moved she was by the ceremony."*
"Dad, THAT WAS GRANDMA!"

I said, "What are you talking about?"

My daughter said, "Remember how grandma would grab both your hands by the wrists, look you straight in the eyes and then talk to you?"

I said, "yes."

"Well, the waitress grabbed both my hands, looked me straight in the eyes and said, "Now Ariella, are you ok with your father getting married? You know he loves you very much and look how happy he is." Then she made a little small talk and after we talked a short while, she left. "Dad, I nearly fell on the floor!"

"I don't even know how she knew my name, let alone grabbing my hands."

"But wait! There's more…She then went up to Adam and Ian." Just FYI, Adam and Ian are my two sons. "Dad, you have to talk to them about what happened."

That next weekend, we had an engagement party for my older son, Adam. It was at that gathering that I had the opportunity to call over my two sons and ask them about the waitress Esther. As soon as I called them over and mentioned the waitresses name, they both went wild. "Oh my God dad! She came up from behind us and meowed!" When my parents would visit and mom would enter the house, to make the kids aware that grandma had arrived, her calling card was always a meow.

Startled, when we both turned around, this waitress looked lovingly at both of us like she knew us and then exclaimed, "I'm so proud of you boys and how handsome you both look in your tuxedo's. Your Dad looks so happy with Kathy. I'm so happy for them and always remember, I love you boys." Then Esther left.

At that point both sons went on and on about the incident. "Dad! That was definitely grandma!"

Here's the point of my story and this entire book… It's an interactive universe, the more you work on yourself, the more the two worlds get close. There is no such thing as death!

Printed in the United States
by Baker & Taylor Publisher Services